Gardening with Colour
at Coton Manor

Gardening with Colour
at Coton Manor

Susie Pasley-Tyler

PIMPERNEL
PRESS LTD
www.pimpernelpress.com

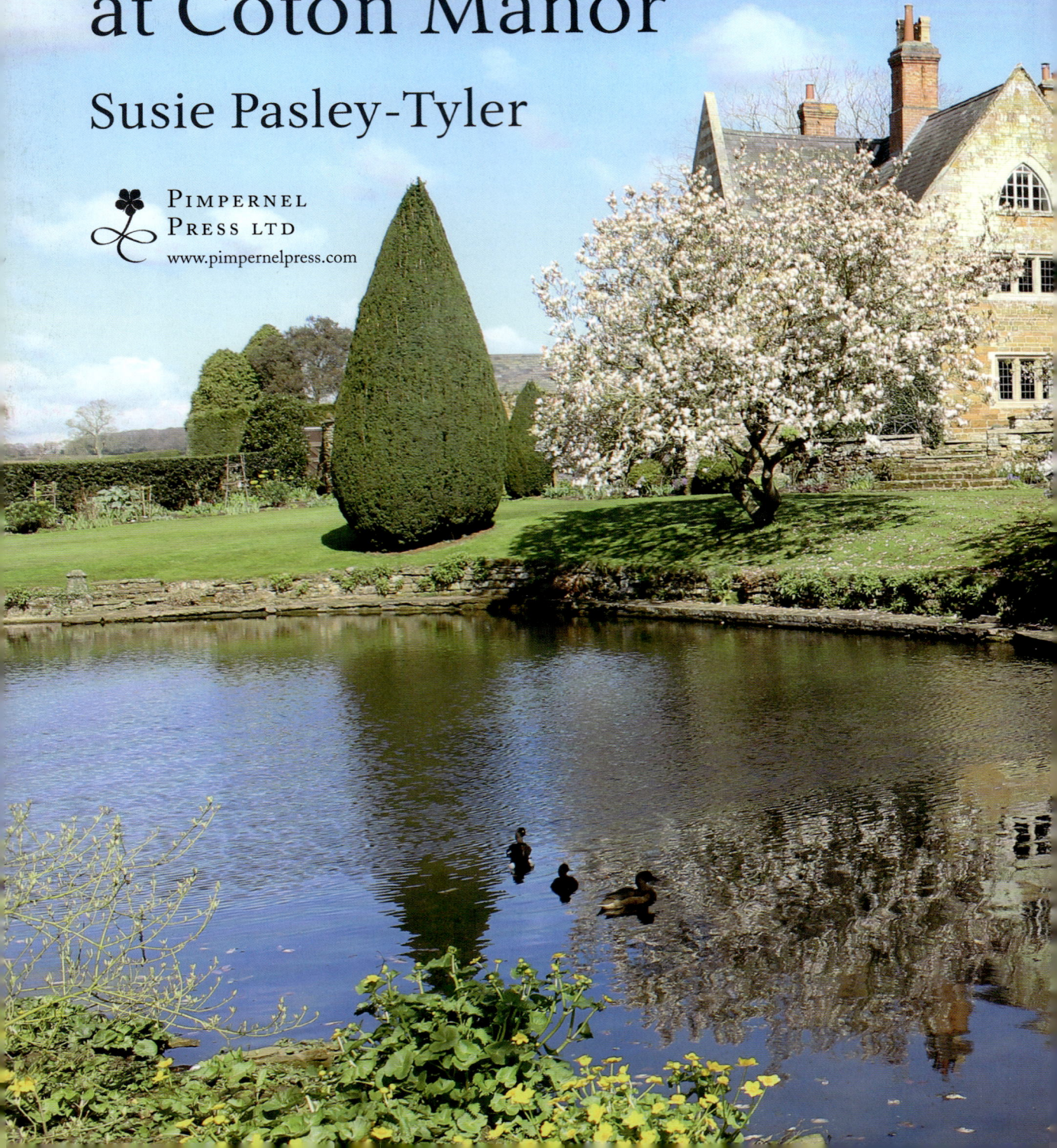

I would like to dedicate this book to my husband, Ian, who introduced me to Coton, to his parents for bequeathing us this wonderful home and garden, and to his grandparents for their inspiration in creating it

Pimpernel Press Limited
www.pimpernelpress.com

Gardening with Colour at Coton Manor
© Pimpernel Press Limited 2024
Text © Susie Pasley-Tyler 2024
Except for Foreword © Andrew Lawson 2024
Photographs and illustrations © Susie Pasley-Tyler 2024
Except for those listed otherwise on page 240
Front cover photograph © Nicola Stocken 2024

A catalogue record for this book is available from the British Library.

Design by Anne Wilson
Typeset in Lunaquete

ISBN 978-1-914902-0-86
Printed and bound in China
By C&C Offset Printing Company Limited
9 8 7 6 5 4 3 2 1

FSC
www.fsc.org
MIX
Paper | Supporting responsible forestry
FSC® C008047

PAGE 1 The Meadow Border in September, featuring crocosmias, dahlias, agastache and verbena
PAGES 2–3 The house and main pond in early April with *Magnolia* × *soulangeana* and *Prunus* 'Shirotae' in flower
RIGHT *Clematis* 'Lemon Beauty' and *Helleborus argutifolius* flanking a stone obelisk

Contents

Foreword by Andrew Lawson

WHEN YOU PICK UP THIS BOOK and start to read, you will soon see that the author has found her passion in life. She simply loves her garden and can't wait to show you the discoveries that she has made. In this book she will lead you through her borders at Coton Manor with a smile on her face. In her garden it has been her delight to put together plants that show off the best of each other. And now she is longing to tell you about them.

Susie Pasley-Tyler came with her husband, Ian, to Coton in Northamptonshire in 1991. He had recently inherited the family home from his parents. At the time neither of them knew much about gardening. But Susie was fired up and didn't look back. She had discovered her mission. Without professional training but by sheer hard work, in winter as well as summer, she has lifted the quality of the garden at Coton to the highest level. She has Ian's administrative support, and they have enjoyed the back-up of a brilliant head gardener, Richard Green, who had started here, fresh from school, in 1979. Together, their greatest delight came in 2019 at the Garden Museum when Coton Manor won 'The Nation's Favourite Garden' award.

Susie says that 'experimenting with colour is my great passion.' Proof of her success with colour can be seen everywhere in the garden and on every page of this book. She delights in the associations of colour in her borders, between the purple-pink flowers of honesty, for instance, and the same hues in the adjacent flower of a cardoon. She looks out for further plants that will extend the family likenesses of colours.

An extreme example, which is sure to have made her laugh, is her solution for the area in which Coton's pet flamingos live. To link with the birds' distinctive pinky-orange plumage, she has chosen gorgeous orange 'Ballerina' tulips in the adjacent borders, with perennials of similar hues to follow in later seasons.

A tulip story that makes Susie smile featured a birthday present from a garden helper, another Sue, who made a secret planting of a beautiful small species tulip to come up as a delightful surprise around the time of her birthday.

Susie Pasley-Tyler's passion for her own garden is highly infectious. Perhaps there should be a health warning that this book will make you want to follow her example and revise all the choices that you have made in your own garden.

The south-east terrace with roses and pots of tender plants in June

Painting of the Rose Garden by Chris Prout

GARDENING WITH COLOUR AT COTON MANOR

Introduction

M Y REASON FOR WRITING THIS BOOK is to try and convey the huge pleasure that gardening has given me in the three decades since 1991 when my husband and I were fortunate enough to inherit his family home and garden at Coton Manor in Northamptonshire. It is an attempt to chart how my passion for gardening has developed, to impart some of the knowledge learnt and mistakes made, and above all to reveal the sheer delight that can be gained from this creative and restorative pastime. Hardly a day passes when I don't find something to prompt a smile in the garden. This is particularly true in late winter and spring when the excitement of seeing the first flowers of winter aconites, snowdrops and hellebores, the primulas appearing or ferns uncoiling, buds bursting on early shrubs, crocus opening in sunshine and new foliage on trees remind us of the magic of nature renewing itself for another season in the garden – a really heartwarming and welcome feeling.

When we found ourselves rather unexpectedly taking over the garden after my mother-in-law's death from a stroke, I had little experience beyond what was needed for a typical narrow London garden. In some ways maybe that was an advantage, because I think I was less daunted than I might have been had I been more knowledgeable. Initially, I had to resort to Latin plant names scribbled by my mother-in-law on old envelopes and garden magazines, together with a few typed lists, to try and work out what plants were in the garden. We inherited two young gardeners, one of whom, Richard Green, is still here, having started at Coton in 1979. However, they had been principally employed helping my father-in-law with mowing, hedge cutting, managing wildlife, repairing waterways and mending machines rather than dealing with borders. I think my mother-in-law decided where plants should go and they would do the work. She was a good friend of Valerie Finnis (aka Lady Scott), who with her husband ran a plant nursery from the Dower House at Boughton House not far away. A lot of the more special plants in the garden had been acquired from this nursery, and I am pleased to say that many of them have survived to this day.

But it did take some time for us to work out what and where everything was. And it was only after two years with the arrival of John Kimball, a keen amateur who had been taught by his grandmother to garden, that I began to understand the most fundamental thing about gardening: the soil. At Coton we are on clay, which has the advantage of retaining nutrients which plants need to thrive, but also has an unfortunate tendency to be too heavy and wet to work on in winter and to bake rock hard and crack in summer unless it is improved. And that is what John taught me to understand. It requires a mixture of farmyard muck, homemade compost, leaf mould and grit or gravel to keep it workable. And the burnt soil underneath a bonfire is a very good soil improver too.

He also taught me the importance of choosing plants for the right soil conditions. We are fortunate to have a soil pH of roughly 6.5, which is just on the acid side of neutral, so we are able to grow most things except for those needing really acid or alkaline soil. However, it is obviously still important to know which plants can cope with dry and damp conditions and those needing sun or preferring shade. I have never had any professional training but have really learnt by trial and error, by reading books and magazines, and, most particularly, by visiting other gardens where you see new plants or plants you already have used in a different context, and invariably come up with ideas which you can translate into your own garden. Over the years we have generously been given many plants, and it gives me so much pleasure to be reminded of those people when I walk round the garden. I should perhaps add here that my own gardening knowledge and experience do not extend to propagation or vegetable and fruit growing, although in the course of our work we supply the nursery with a considerable amount of plant material for division, bulbs that we have dug up and seeds that we have collected. I am fortunate to have an excellent team of propagators in the nursery, who also take care of vegetable growing for me.

However, had I been presented with the blank canvas that my husband's grandparents found in the 1920s when they moved to Coton, I would not have known where to begin, and it is both to them for their inspiration in choosing the site and their skill in laying out the garden, and to my parents-in-law for extending their good work and increasing the plant repertoire, that we really owe our gratitude. In effect, we have been icing the cake that had already been baked, and it has been such fun to carry on with what they bequeathed us. In addition, we have been fortunate to have some wonderful helpers in the garden since the start of our tenure here. In particular, we owe so much to Richard Green, our Head Gardener, who has worked at Coton since he left school in 1979. Apart from looking after the structure – the lawns, hedges, trees, water features, birds and animals – he created the rill that runs between the Old Orchards, the Herb Garden which he designed and has managed over the years, the area above the Canal Run where the semi-circular benches provide a welcome spot for visitors to sit and enjoy the view, and the Wildflower Meadow which he has tended since its inception. I also have a brilliant team of part-timers who help me with the planting in the beds and borders, without whom the garden wouldn't look the way it does. And that it is not to forget the team in the nursery whose invaluable work provides a wonderful range of plants both to tempt visitors and to use in the garden.

I hope that readers who may not already be gardeners will be encouraged by my experience to find how much pleasure gardening can provide on so many different levels. It is clearly good exercise and it can also be uplifting for mind and spirit. Rather like singing, it can be totally absorbing to the exclusion of everyday worries and concerns. The great thing about gardening is that one never stops learning so it never becomes boring. No two seasons are alike; there are always new plants to try out. It is a totally subjective art form, and compared with any form of interior decoration it is far more forgiving as it is easy to move things to a better position at very little cost if they are not happy. Above all, it is a game of patience. The pleasure is in anticipation: looking forward to the results of work done six months earlier or waiting several years to see a shrub or tree mature. And seeing the results of that wait is what makes it really rewarding.

This book describes in some detail how we garden at Coton Manor, how the garden has evolved since we started here over thirty years ago, and the focus that I have in my head for its many and varied sites. It reveals both triumphs and failures, and I hope will convey to the reader the pleasure to be gained from becoming somewhat addicted as I have. There are a number of chapters dealing with different aspects of our gardening work, so you can scan and seek out the headings that interest you or read straight through the book as you choose.

Brief History

As I have mentioned, we are the third generation of the family to live and garden at Coton. My husband's grandparents purchased the house and land in 1926. He was Harold Bryant, an Englishman who had lived in America for many years, and his wife, Elizabeth, was American. In his fifties he decided to return to England because he wanted to hunt with foxhounds and the Pytchley Hunt drew him to Northamptonshire. There is a manor house at Coton recorded in the Domesday Book; it had different owners and tenants and probably several rebuilds through the centuries until 1645, when it was razed to the ground the night before the Battle of Naseby by Cromwell's New Model Army, who camped in Coton and the two neighbouring villages before the battle took place five miles away.

The house that they bought in 1926 had been rebuilt on this site in 1662 during the Restoration as a farmhouse. They extended and restored the house to its current form and created the garden. The only garden belonging to the farmhouse was a vegetable patch which was bounded by a holly hedge to protect it from farm animals – hence the rather curiously positioned holly hedge at right angles to the house. To develop a garden from sloping farmland bereft of trees, they created terraces round the south-west and south-east sides of the house. They planted a shelter belt of white willows (*Salix alba*) and some significant trees, including a tulip tree (*Liriodendron tulipifera*), a black walnut (*Juglans nigra*), a copper beech (*Fagus sylvatica* f. *purpurea*) and many more, all of which we now enjoy in their fully mature state. The garden is blessed with a spring-fed pond, and they skilfully created the Water Garden from a stream flowing from the pond. A rill was made from another outlet from the pond running between two orchards, which they planted with apple, pear and damson trees, leading down the slope to the only flat part of the garden, where they laid out two grass tennis courts. They also built the Stable Yard with a groom's cottage (now restaurant), several stables and sundry related buildings. And below this area they laid out the Kitchen Garden. One of the things that they couldn't have realised in the 1920s when they created the garden was how effectively it anchors the house. Wherever you are, you can always glimpse the house in the distance, even from the Wildflower Meadow and field beyond. I think there is something reassuring about this, particularly for visitors in need of a cup of tea.

RIGHT ABOVE Nineteenth-century painting of the farmhouse known then as Coton Grange
RIGHT BELOW The house, restored to a manor house, in the 1920s

My husband's parents inherited the house in the 1950s. The garden required a huge amount of work following the war when minimal help had been available. During the next two decades they gradually restored and extended it and eventually opened to the public in 1969. During this period they improved borders, created more waterways, made the Woodland Garden, and introduced a considerable number of wildfowl, including flamingos. They also added the garden room to the house, which has been a wonderful asset for summer events, including our Garden School courses.

For those readers who are not familiar with it, I will try to describe briefly the constituent parts which together create what so many visitors remark on as its indefinable atmosphere. To give some idea of the scale, the garden is approximately 2.4 ha/6 acres, while the Wildflower Meadow covers 1.2 ha/ 3 acres and the Bluebell Wood is 2 ha/5 acres. Many people say that they find the garden therapeutic, and nothing could give me more pleasure than to know that. The stone house enjoys glorious views on three sides. The land falls away and there is a lovely view down to the 36-ha/90-acre Ravensthorpe Reservoir on the south-east side, a typical Northamptonshire scene of a valley and rising ground to the south-west and farmland to the north-west. Most of the garden faces south-west. Situated two-thirds of the way down a steepish hill, it is fed by springs so there are quite a number of ponds, streams, pools, canals and rills throughout the garden. Mature trees and strong yew and holly hedges lend definition to the different areas which, partly due to the slope, only reveal themselves gradually to the visitor. There are many colourful borders in the sunnier parts of the garden, but also areas of quieter, more intimate planting and a number of large green spaces which allow the eyes to rest.

1   The Entrance Yard
2   The Morning Room Bed
3   The South-West Terrace
4   The Poop Deck Beds
5   The South-East Terrace
6   The Holly Hedge Border
7   The Alpine Terrace
8   The Rose Garden
9   The Woodland Garden
10 The Statue Bed
11 The Main Pond
12 The Water Garden
13 The Bog Garden
14 The Mediterranean Bank
15 The Old Orchards
16 The Dells
17 The Meadow Border
18 The Wildflower Meadow
19 The Bluebell Wood
20 The Blue and Yellow Border
21 The Red Border
22 The Midsummer Border
23 The Rose Bank
24 The Herb Garden
25 The Gravel Garden
26 The Italian Garden
27 The Acacia Border

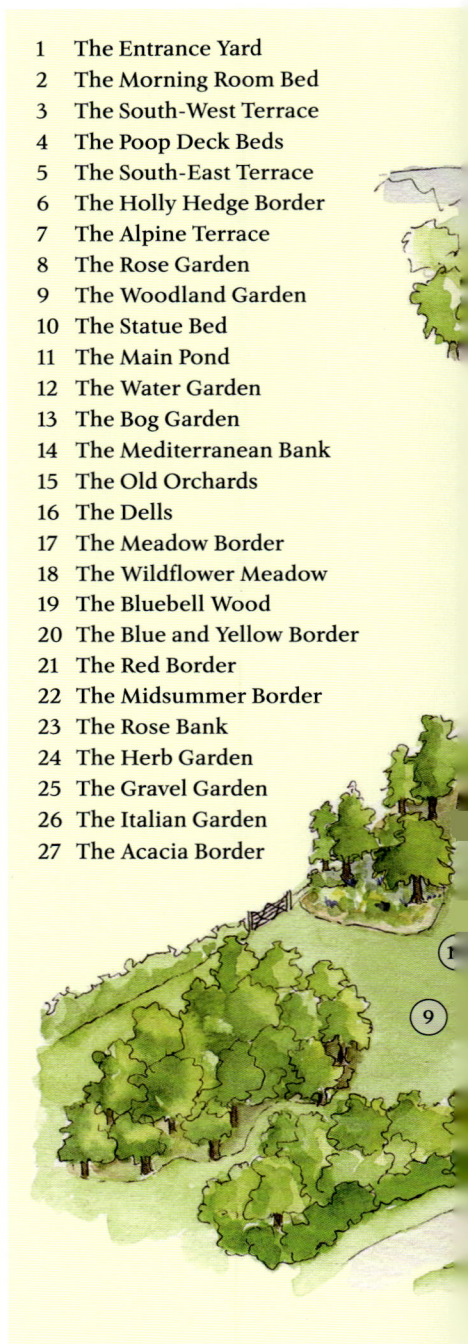

Map showing the areas of the garden featured in the book

The Use of Colour in the Garden

ONE OF THE MOST frequent comments from visitors to the garden is about the use of colour. Over the years it has become a major preoccupation and pleasure of mine to experiment and play with colours in the beds and borders. And it is immensely satisfying when I get it right. My initial interest was triggered by the realisation that in one of the larger borders we had inherited there was a resonance between the silver foliage of the cardoon, *Cynara cardunculus*, and the purple-pink flowers of honesty, *Lunaria annua*, which had seeded itself in a random way. In retrospect, I realize that this appreciation of the extent to which one colour can enhance another and add an extra dimension to a planting scheme gave me the inspiration to pick up the colour of the honesty and run with it. So I started with tulips, followed by alliums, astrantias, roses, clematis, penstemons, salvias, dahlias and cleomes in shades of this colour, which to my eye is neither purple nor pink but somewhere between the two. Its repetition throughout the season then became the backbone of the border. The grey and silver foliage already existed in a more subdued way in the form of echinops and a tree peony, *Paeonia delavayi* × (× *suffruticosa*), and we have since added to this effect with the introduction of the smoky tones of *Sedum* (syn. *Hylotelephium*) 'Matrona', the grey leaves of *Stachys byzantina* 'Big Ears' and the more silvery foliage of *Romneya coulteri*. It also taught me that repetition of colour is restful to the eye as it makes this connection, rather than becoming confused by a myriad of different colours. Naturally, there needs to be a

The Acacia Border in September

The small diagram of the colour wheel shows the difference between the warm and cool colours. The larger diagram gives a clearer idea of complementary (opposite) colours and harmonious (adjacent) colours.

supporting cast of sympathetic colours to create a more interesting effect. So, here – known for historical reasons as the Acacia Border – I have used a mixture of blue, pink and purple (adjacent on the colour wheel) with white; silver, smoky grey and dark red foliage provide a contrasting foil. In this way I discovered the effectiveness of limiting and repeating colours within a border.

There are no absolute rights and wrongs about the use of colour in a garden because it is a subjective exercise and people see and enjoy colours in different ways. It is a physiological fact that women have more cones in their eyes, while men have more rods. Theories arising from this difference suggest that this may increase women's ability to discern the nuances between colours, while in the case of men it can increase their ability to see more clearly in the dark. This perhaps goes some way to explaining why women may tend to favour softer colour schemes and men may prefer the use of bolder colours. But the colour wheel is a useful tool to remind oneself of the general principle that adjacent colours are generally harmonious and opposite colours create a contrast. In my experience, successful colour schemes require a balance between the two, erring on the side of harmony rather than contrast.

From the experience of the Acacia Border I have learnt to create a colour palette in my head for various beds around the garden. It is immensely satisfying and huge fun when acquiring a new plant to have an instinct as to where the flower colour would look right with the

surrounding planting, provided the soil and light conditions are also favourable, rather than randomly putting it in a vacant space. It has also taught me about the different qualities that colours evoke. This has been a spur to enhancing a different feel or mood while walking round the garden by varying the planting between more vibrant and colourful areas and quieter ones, thereby contributing to its overall ambience. Over the years, I have been creating distinctive colour schemes in different borders, but like everything else to do with gardening (unlike interior decoration), it requires constant editing. A garden never stands still. Plants outgrow their space, need to be reduced or replaced; positions need to be found for new plants, and generally there is always room for improvement. One can never be complacent that any area is 'finished' and hence, once bitten by the gardening bug, one can never become bored.

If starting a border from scratch, it is a good opportunity to develop a feeling for the sort of colours that would seem to be sympathetic to that space, bearing in mind the background and surrounding foliage or hard surfaces. More often people find themselves renovating and

ABOVE LEFT *Allium* 'Purple Sensation' and *Clematis integrifolia*
ABOVE RIGHT *Dahlia* 'Le Baron' and *Cleome hassleriana* 'Violet Queen'

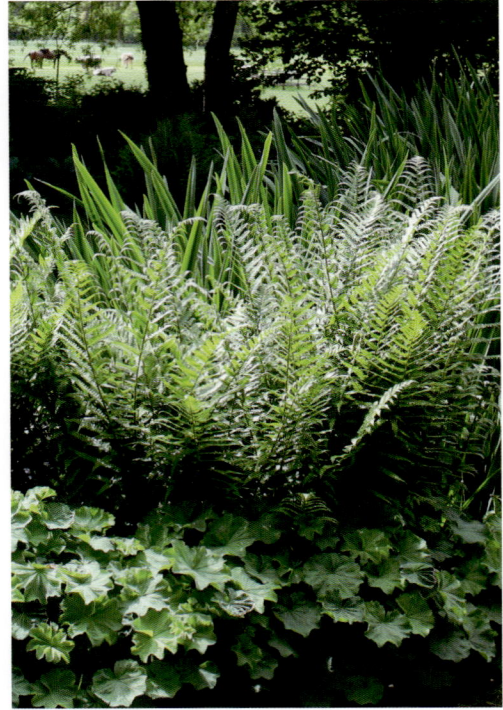

improving an existing border. Then it might be a good idea to build up a colour palette drawn from one or more of the existing plants or shrubs. I shall consider the composition of a border in the following chapter. It is a very complex process, and I am dealing with colour first because it is what most people notice first. However, it is only when considerations of structure, texture, shape, foliage, light conditions, the disposition and logistics of placing plants and so many other aspects are taken into account that the effect of a colour palette can be shown to greatest advantage.

It is perhaps worth pausing here to consider the qualities of different colours and how they work in the form of plants. Very few plants are single coloured. They are usually quite complex and may combine several colours either in their petals, stamens and stems or in their leaves. One of the things that delights my eye is to play with details – for example, to place a tulip such as 'Elegant Lady', which is creamy yellow suffused with a subtle shade of deep pink, adjacent to the exquisite pale yellow flowers of *Paeonia mlokosewitchii* with its corresponding deep pink stamens and stems. Both flower at the same time, and by putting the two together, you create the value of three plants, if only for a brief ephemeral moment – but that is what gardening is all about. Another example is a small bed backed by an Irish yew, where we have a planting of white flowers, amongst which are several *Rosa* 'Jacqueline du Pré' with its distinctive red stamens, which I chose to pick up the tiny red flowers of *Tropaeolum speciosum* growing up the yew.

When asked which is my favourite colour in the garden, I have no hesitation in saying 'green'. It is, of course, the dominant colour in nature – in trees, hedges, foliage and grass – and it is profoundly restful. It comes in so many shades from blue-green through to yellow-green. A composition of greens, such as the green flowers of *Helleborus argutifolius* together with the elegant fronds of a polystichum fern and a libertia with its linear leaves, can be as pleasing, if not more so, than a colourful grouping in a border. This is in part due to the effect of the different greens, but also to the contrasting textures and shapes of the foliage and flowers.

In spring the greens are most vibrant, and in many ways there is less need at this stage for flower colour as the range provides such a feast for the eyes. Watching ferns uncoil is a special delight at this time of year. Indeed, the number of plants with green flowers has increased in recent years and they are worth seeking out. In addition to the winter-flowering hellebores, there are primulas, viridiflora tulips, euphorbia, tellima, alchemilla, astrantia, echinacea, kniphofia and zinnia spanning the seasons. But it is foliage which provides the most wonderful

LEFT *Astrantia major* subsp. *involucrata* 'Shaggy' (left); foliage of iris, ferns and alchemilla (right)
ABOVE *Hosta* 'Halcyon' and *Tellima grandiflora* (left); *Euphorbia wulfenii* subsp. *characias*, *Clematis* 'Guernsey Cream' and *Lunaria annua* (right)

foil and embellishment in planting schemes. It is always worth remembering that while plants have a limited flowering period, foliage by and large lasts from spring to autumn or even longer. Some plants – such as baptisia, thermopsis and amsonia – still retain good foliage after flowering has finished, others less so, while quite a number of others will benefit from being completely cut back to renew them. Foliage comes in different shades, shapes, sizes and variegations, and its capacity to be light absorbent or reflective also varies. All these aspects contribute to the richness of a planting scheme. Finally, I would say that green is the most soothing and subtle colour in the garden while never being flamboyant.

From observing what visitors buy in our nursery and what they remark on in the garden, I think plants with blue flowers are probably the most sought after, particularly among women. It is hard to imagine a garden without blue. But it is a recessive colour, which can disappear in the distance, and in its more sombre shades it can appear to give a melancholy effect. There is such a huge range of blue flowering plants from pale to dark, verging on aqua at one extreme

and on purple at another, and there is royal blue or what some might describe as 'true blue', which stands out on its own (unlike most blues). Sadly, there are precious few plants in this colour – *Meconopsis betonicifolia*, *Omphalodes* 'Cherry Ingram', *Brunnera macrophylla*, some delphiniums, *Commelina tuberosa*, *Salvia patens*, *Ceratostigma plumbaginoides* and *C. willmottianum*, to name a few in this garden. Not a huge number if you are attempting to span the flowering season. Blue is really shown to advantage against orange and yellow and to a lesser extent alongside shades of pink and white. Personally, I would find a border with predominantly blue flowers unsatisfying. So, much as I love blue flowers, I regard them as part of a supporting cast in a planting scheme.

LEFT *Clematis heracleifolia* 'Cassandra', *Verbena bonariensis*, *Rudbeckia* 'Goldsturm' and *Dahlia* 'Shooting Star'
ABOVE (CLOCKWISE FROM TOP LEFT) *Meconopsis × sheldonii* 'Lingholm'; *Delphinium* 'Volkerfrieden';
Omphalodes cappadocica 'Cherry Ingram'; *Iris sibirica* 'Silver Edge'

Purple can also be recessive, but it has a depth and intensity that makes it stand out. A plant such as *Salvia* 'Amistad' makes a big statement and is also invaluable as it will flower over a long period. I think it is interesting the way blue is used rather loosely to describe some plants which I would regard as being more akin to purple. This is a slightly grey area in nomenclature as clearly people perceive colours differently. For example, most of the herbaceous salvias originating from eastern parts of Europe, such as forms of *S. nemorosa*, *S. × sylvestris* and *S. verticillata* that flower in early summer, I would describe as mauve or purple, but they are often called blue. Both purple and blue work well when coupled with yellow and orange, although in colour wheel terms orange and blue are opposites, as are purple and yellow – showing that contrasts can be pleasing.

ABOVE *Nepeta subsessilis*, *Salvia × sylvestris* 'May Night', *Achillea* 'Moonshine' and *Lupinus* 'Chandelier'
RIGHT (CLOCKWISE FROM TOP LEFT) *Salvia* 'Amistad'; *Iris ensata* and *Alchemilla mollis*; *Verbena bonariensis*, *Crocosmia* 'Zambesi' and *Agastache* 'Blue Fortune'; *Clematis* 'Jackmanii Superba' and *Rosa* 'Ghislaine de Féligonde'

RIGHT *Rosa gallica* 'Versicolor' (syn. *R. mundi*) and *Salvia × sylvestris* 'May Night' OPPOSITE (CLOCKWISE FROM TOP LEFT) *Salvia involucrata*; *Geranium sanguineum* var. *striatum*; *Morina longifolia*, *Achillea* 'Cerise Queen' and *Rosa* 'De Rescht'; *Diascia fetcaniensis*; *R.* 'Lady Emma Hamilton' and *Clematis heracleifolia* 'Cassandra'

Pink is another colour that comes in so many different tones and shades. At its deepest, which I would describe as purple-pink or magenta, it is very much a stand-out colour in its own right. This is the colour which I have majored on in the Acacia Border described earlier. There it appears in the form of *Lunaria annua*, tulips 'Negrita' and 'Curly Sue', *Allium* 'Purple Sensation', *Clematis* 'Alionushka', *C. flammula* 'Sweet Summer Love', *C. viticella* 'Odoriba' and *C.* 'Margot Koster', *Rosa* 'Tour de Malakoff', *R.* 'De Rescht' and *R.* 'Reine des Violettes', *Cleome* 'Violet Queen', *Dahlia* 'Cornish Ruby', *D.* 'Le Baron' and *Salvia* 'Magenta Dream'.

There are many roses in strong rich pink, which conveys a sense of warmth. However, the paler shades of pink tend to perform more of a supporting role in colour schemes. To my eye there is a clear distinction between the softness of blue-pinks and the stronger yellow-pinks, and I don't think the two mix well. Shades of apricot-pink create a subtle effect and can look dazzling offset with blue. The range of pinks is huge, and it is probably the colour which appears most frequently around the garden in its different shades, mostly in harmonious – but sometimes in deliberately contrasting – colour schemes.

There is something exquisite about the richness of what I would call true red, by which I mean a pure red that betrays a hint of neither blue nor yellow. It never fails to make a strong impact. To show it to its greatest advantage, I like to combine red with lots of green and some pale yellow. In one very long border, which is mostly viewed sideways on, I inherited several roses in an orange-red, namely 'Fred Loads' and 'Scarlet Queen Elizabeth'. My first instinct was to remove them, but after a year or two I began to appreciate their value. The foliage of other plants has lost its vibrancy by midsummer in this particular border, which is backed by a glittery holly hedge, and the rest of the planting is in relatively pale shades, so the colour of these roses holds it together and gives it definition. Instead of getting rid of them, I introduced more reds at a lower height to span the seasons, in the form of alstroemeria, shrubby salvias, penstemons, fuchsias and schizostylis (now known as hesperantha) to create a rhythm of red highlighting the paler colours.

ABOVE The Holly Hedge Border in September
RIGHT (CLOCKWISE FROM TOP) *Rosa* 'Dublin Bay', *Geum* 'Mrs Bradshaw', *Lupinus* 'Chandelier' and *Verbascum chaixii* in the Red Border; *Papaver* 'Beauty of Livermere'; *Dahlia* 'Bishop of Llandaff'

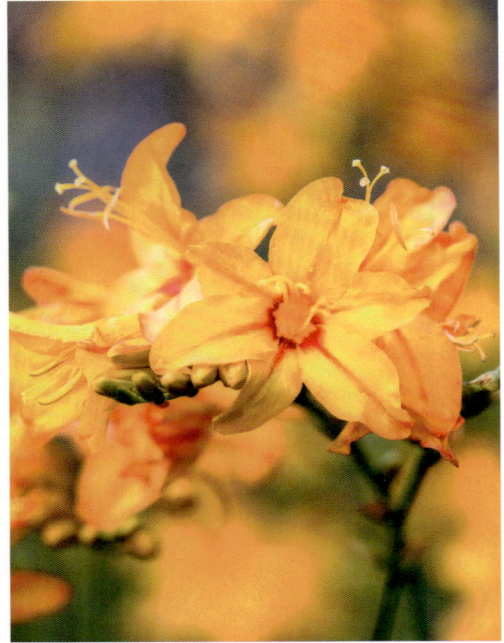

ABOVE *Primula bulleyana*
and *Meconopsis × sheldonii*
'Lingholm' (left); *Crocosmia*
'Zambesi' (right)
RIGHT *Dahlia* 'Glorie van
Noordwijk'
OPPOSITE *Helenium*
'Zimbelstern' (left); *Lupinus*
'Chandelier' (right)

Orange, like yellow, can be a controversial colour in the garden for some people. Many women abhor orange and are not too enthusiastic about yellow. But in gardening, provided there is space, I think there is a place for most plants and colours. It is a question of choosing the right context. Orange is useful because it stands out well from a distance. Another virtue is how glorious it can look with blue and green. I find it joyous and it gives me huge pleasure in the garden. Most of the plants we have in shades of orange, apart from tulips and geums, tend to perform in the second part of the summer season and have generous flowering periods, such as heleniums, kniphofias and crocosmias. In addition, we now have a number of roses and dahlias in interesting shades varying from pale apricot to deep orange.

Yellow is particularly effective in spring and late summer, but in its stronger shades can be quite glaring in high summer, which is when I prefer to use its paler forms. Unfortunately, there are frustratingly few plants with pale yellow flowers from midsummer onwards – *Nepeta govaniana*, *Phlomis russeliana*, *Digitalis lutea*, *Alstroemeria* 'Yellow Friendship', *Kniphofia* 'Percy's Pride', *Rosa* 'Imogen' and *Salvia* 'Creme Caramel' are a few that I use. However, because, unlike blue, yellow draws the eye, it can be used to good effect with just green, and, of course, it is shown to particular advantage contrasted with purple and blue.

White does not feature on the colour wheel, but I couldn't contemplate being without it in the garden. Although I am not one to go for single colour schemes, there are a few shady areas in our garden where I just use white because it works well against the dark green background of both yew and holly, especially in shady conditions. It can be glaring in high summer, but looks wonderful in the softer light of late summer and autumn. Like red, white can be effective in highlighting a border planting, especially in the lower light levels of September and October. There is a small bed opposite the end of our long Holly Hedge Border, surrounded by yew and holly and under the shade of a huge tulip tree (*Liriodendron tulipifera*) where the sun seldom penetrates. Here I grow *Viola septentrionalis*, *Geranium maccrorhizum* 'Whiteness', *Ranunculus aconitifolius* 'Flore Pleno', *Artemisia lactiflora* 'Guizhou Group', *Aster divaricatus* (syn. *Eurybia divaricata*), *Fuchsia magellanica* 'Hawkshead', *Anemone* × *hybrida* 'Honorine Jobert' and *Eupatorium rugosum*. Despite the lack of sunshine and dryness caused by the surrounding hedges, this area always has something in flower to lighten up the shade.

I have tried to describe above my interpretation of colour in a garden context, but I would like to stress how very subjective this is. As you may have gathered, experimenting with colour is my great passion and gives me endless pleasure and satisfaction. In the next few pages, I will give a more detailed description of how I have developed colour themes in borders that were already established and in some that have been created from scratch, using the theories I have gradually taught myself through trial and error over three decades. Sometimes I have to label a border by its dominant colour for want of any other description. However, I would like to think that the borders are not too obviously colour co-ordinated and that their colour composition can be appreciated at a subliminal level. I have contrived to create varied colour schemes round the garden which evoke different moods and ensure that they reach their 'best moment' at different times.

It is inevitable that the following descriptions of the different parts of the garden include quite long lists of plants. They are, after all, the component elements or instruments which create the effect. I have attempted to list plants roughly in the order in which they flower through the season. One of the most difficult things in organising a border is succession: keeping it in continuous flower. There will always be one or possibly two periods in the season when a border might be deemed to be at its best, but there is still a need to keep the performance going in between these peak times. It takes years of practice and experience to gain the knowledge about the relative habits and flowering periods of all the plants in a garden, especially a large one like ours, and even then the weather can undermine their performance, as we discovered in the extreme heat and consequent drought of the summer of 2022. The lists may seem extensive in one or two of the larger borders, but they are far from comprehensive; the appendix at the end of this book has more complete lists of the main borders and beds discussed below and elsewhere.

ABOVE LEFT *Galanthus plicatus* ex 'Coton Manor'
ABOVE RIGHT *Anemone × hybrida* 'Honorine Jobert'
LEFT *Magnolia stellata* and flamingos in the Goose Park

THE SOUTH-WEST TERRACE

I have already described how my inspiration to attempt a colour scheme derived from the juxtaposition of the silver-leafed cardoon and the simple honesty in the Acacia Border. This border sits at right angles below the entrance terrace to the garden, and it is fortunate that its predominant colour of magenta or purple-pink is by chance echoed in the flowers of *Rosa multiflora* 'Platyphylla' (Seven Sisters' rose), which adorns the walls on this side of the house. I have therefore repeated it and its supporting colours on the terrace, principally with *Erysimum* 'Bowles's Mauve', *Syringa meyeri* 'Palibin', *Geranium sanguineum* 'Elke', *Penstemon* 'Countess of Dalkeith' and *P.* 'Raven', *Salvia* 'Lalarsha', *S.* 'Nachtvlinder' and *S. microphylla* 'Pink Blush', *Clematis viticella* 'Madame Julia Correvon' and *C. viticella* 'Odoriba', and *Dahlia* 'Purple Gem'. These deep pinks and purples are in turn set off by the silver foliage of *Artemisia nutans*, *A. canescens* and *Senecio viravira* and the dark red leaves of *Heuchera* 'Obsidian'. So, as you enter the garden, if you look left and right you may perceive a link between the colours in the Acacia Border below and those on the terrace.

OPPOSITE View showing seventeenth-century facade of the house

ABOVE *Rosa multiflora* 'Platyphylla' (Seven Sisters' rose) on the south-west terrace

LEFT *Clematis viticella* 'Madame Julia Correvon' and *Agapanthus* 'Doctor Brouwer'

THE HOLLY HEDGE BORDER

Coming round the corner of the house on to the south-east terrace, you are immediately confronted by a long and narrow border backed by the holly hedge which is at right angles to the house. This is the visitor's first view of this border and arguably the most effective angle from which to appreciate it. Due to its shallow depth (1.8 m/6 ft) and long length (32 m/105 ft) and very dominant position, it is immensely challenging to manage, not least because most of the border is in full sun but the last quarter is in shade. This is where the roses 'Fred Loads' and 'Scarlet Queen Elizabeth' were when we took over the garden, together with *Fuchsia magellanica* 'Mrs Popple', which we also retained. Most of the plants here were in pastel shades which looked fine in spring with their vibrant foliage, but less so from midsummer onwards when greens tend to merge into duller shades.

Gradually it dawned on me that there was a value in retaining the scarlet roses because the colour stands out against the glittery reflective effect of the holly hedge. So I increased their number and spaced them out, but kept the quieter components of blues, pinks, whites and mauves. The roses stand at about 1.2–1.5 m/4–5 ft high, so over the years we have added other red flowering plants at an intermediate and lower level. These include plantings of a red alstroemeria, *Salvia* 'Silke's Red', *Penstemon* 'King George' and *P.* 'Windsor Red', *Lobelia tupa* and *Hesperantha major*, which are repeated down its length. This lends definition to the border and helps to create a sense of rhythm. There are a number of blues in repeated plantings of polemoniums, baptisia, herbaceous clematis, delphiniums, agapanthus, aconitums and asters; pinks and mauves in the form of *Tulipa* 'Finola', *Hesperis matronalis*, *Stachys macrantha*, *Allium cristophii*, *Salvia verticillata* 'Purple Rain', pink *Rosa* 'Ispahan', *Salvia* 'Peter Vidgeon' and *Sedum* (syn. *Hylotelephium*) *spectabile*. Towards the end of June and into July there is a spectacular display of roses and delphiniums, while in August the agapanthus hold centre stage, with articulation from the reds of penstemons and salvias. But it was with the introduction of three groups of a beautiful pale pink dahlia called 'Allan Sparkes' that this border finally achieved the effect I was seeking. The contrast of the scarlet and pink at intervals down the border makes it spectacular in the later part of the season. And in September this effect is enhanced by the white of *Anemone* × *hybrida* 'Honorine Jobert', *Cimicifuga racemosa*, *Nicotiana sylvestris* and the second flowering of roses 'Jacqueline du Pré' and 'Iceberg'. It is a border that starts off quietly and reaches a crescendo in August and September.

RIGHT ABOVE View showing the juxtaposition of the Holly Hedge Border to the house
RIGHT BELOW The Holly Hedge Border in early summer with *Rosa* 'Gloire de Dijon' in foreground
OVERLEAF The Holly Hedge Border in September (highlighted with scarlets and pinks)

THE ROSE GARDEN

Moving further along the terrace brings you to the Rose Garden. This area is composed of five different beds, plus a central quartered circle of four beds intersected by brick paths. When we arrived, the central beds were filled with 140 roses, with peonies at the central corners and *Stachys lanata* around the outer edges, but there were no roses in the surrounding beds. I gradually planted more roses in the outlying beds and left the quartered circle as we found it during the 1990s. However, by 2006 I had become tired of replacing roses suffering from rose replant disease, needing constant deadheading and only flowering for a limited time; the stachys looked good only in the early part of the season. So we decided to take everything out. We removed and retained the topsoil, got rid of approximately 45 cm/18 inches of subsoil, and replaced the topsoil improved with fresh soil, our own compost and a substantial amount of gravel to help the drainage. We then selected a range of plants which could manage with minimal watering, supporting and feeding. The inner paths were lined with a silver form of lavender, initially *Lavandula* 'Sawyers', replaced since with *L.* 'Silver Sands'. We prune it at least twice a year, so it doesn't flower but gives a silver definition to the edge of the paths. The evergreen shrub *Phillyrea angustifolia* was planted at each of the central corners, with somewhat reduced replantings of *Paeonia* 'Sarah Bernhardt' and *P.* 'Duchesse de Nemours' behind them. I absolutely love herbaceous peonies, but I do have reservations about placing them in a frontal position anywhere because in our garden at least their foliage does tend to deteriorate as summer progresses. Interestingly, as I write in 2022 at the end of the hottest summer I can recall, it is the first time that peony foliage has survived intact and

The Rose Garden in late June

reached the autumn displaying its wonderful golden colour. Another reason for removing the mass of roses was because the main rooms of the house look out on this part of the garden, and I wanted to replant with more continuous flowering in summer and some shrub structure for the winter.

With *Rosa* 'Cornelia' in two of the surrounding beds, I took my cue from this strong pink, which I would describe as being on the yellow side of pink. I then added plants in pale blue, white and dark red. I chose dark red because in summer we fill the terrace outside our garden room, which is effectively in the Rose Garden, with a range of pots of regal and ivy leaf pelargoniums, many of which are dark red or have dark red detailing. Initially, we planted *Knautia macedonica* in this colour in each of the four beds, but after a few years of having to stake and endlessly deadhead it, we abandoned this and have since planted

ABOVE The Rose Garden with tulips in May
RIGHT (CLOCKWISE FROM TOP LEFT) *Paeonia mlokosewitchi*; *Rosa* 'Little White Pet'; *R.* 'Cornelia' and *Eryngium* × *oliverianum*; *R.* 'Deep Secret' and *Acidanthera bicolor*

R. 'Deep Secret', which is a wonderful repeat-flowering tall rose with dark red flowers and a delicious scent. We had already introduced a group of three *R.* 'Little White Pet' into each of the four beds about six years after removing the previous roses. And we have now also added *R.* 'The Fairy' into all four beds. With the addition of 'Deep Secret' and 'The Fairy' in each bed and at least another twenty roses in the surrounding beds, we feel we can still just get away with describing this whole area as the Rose Garden. Initially, after replanting, we tried calling it the Old Rose Garden. But I kept on being asked where all the old roses were. It's fair to say that some of them would qualify as 'old', but perhaps not all. So we reverted to the Rose Garden.

The season starts off with tulips in dark red and pale yellow, the former selected to create a contrast and the latter to harmonize with the pale yellow *Paeonia mlokosewitschii* and a *Rosa banksiae* 'Lutea' which has sadly now died. In the quartered circle we plant tulips 'Black Hero' and 'Elegant Lady', repeating 'Elegant Lady' combined with the dark red tulip 'Havran' in the other beds. There are generous plantings of *Erysimum* 'Constant Cheer' in each of the four beds; its curious but effective combination of pink with hints of orange and

yellow echoes both the pink of *R*. 'Cornelia' and the tinge of yellow in *R*. 'Phyllis Bide' over the archway leading to the Woodland Garden, and a similar tone in *R*. 'Ghislaine de Féligonde' in a neighbouring bed. This erysimum has the virtue of flowering for a long time in spring, and its colour is then picked up by *Diascia vigilis*, *Salvia* 'Penny's Smile' and Cleome 'Cherry Queen' and, towards the end of summer, in a quieter form by *Sedum* (syn. *Hylotelephium*) 'Matrona'. *Iris pallida* 'Argentea Variegata' is the first pale blue to flower, followed by *Campanula lactiflora*, *Eryngium bourgatii*, *Salvia* 'African Skies', *Caryopteris × clandonensis* 'Heavenly Blue' and *Agapanthus* 'Blue Moon'. White is found in the flowers of *Libertia grandiflora* (syn. *L. chilensis*), *Geranium renardii*, *Orlaya grandiflora*, *Paeonia* 'Duchesse de Nemours', *R*. 'Little White Pet', a white form of *Agapanthus africanus* and the Abyssinian gladiolus, *Acidanthera bicolor*. The dark red marking in the white gladiolus connects with the beautiful dark red *Antirrhinum* 'Black Prince' and, of course, with *R*. 'Deep Secret'. These four colours are echoed in the flowers in the surrounding beds. Lavender, artemisia, *Convolvulus cneorum*, *Euphorbia myrsinites*, *Stachys byzantina* 'Big Ears' and *Senecio viravira* continue the silver/grey theme with dark red leaf forms of heuchera and *Sedum* 'Bertram Anderson' planted throughout for contrast.

This part of the garden is pretty colourful throughout the season, but is probably at its best in September when the caryopteris and late flowering agapanthus add their pale blue to the pink, dark red and white, while the roses are doing their second flowering.

The Rose Garden in September showing *Agapanthus* 'Blue Moon', *Sedum matrona* and *Cleome hassleriana* 'Cherry Queen' in flower in the foreground

THE MEDITERRANEAN BANK

Situated adjacent to the bottom of the Water Garden and above the Old Orchards, this steep bank was planted with herbs in my parents-in-law's time. In 1994, after removing a very long and decrepit chicken shed from the lower part of the Kitchen Garden, we decided to use that space to create a more formal Herb Garden. This enabled me to remove the herbs from the steep bank, where they had never looked very impressive, and gave me the opportunity to think how we should replant. As it is sheltered and faces south, Mediterranean plants seemed a sensible option. So after adding two tons of gravel to improve drainage and supporting the soil with wooden sleepers, we proceeded to plant forms of rosemary, euphorbia, cistus, iris, thyme, eryngium, lavender, phlomis and agapanthus, but with no particular thought about colour. It remained like this for a number of years. On the right-hand side of this steep bank was a large hedge of *Rhododendron ponticum*. It had been cut back at some stage to allow a pathway through from the lower part of the Water Garden. However, every year the rhododendron grew to the extent that the pathway narrowed and it was challenging to navigate, particularly on a wet day. So we decided to remove the rhododendron from the bank and retain the lower part below the path, which now forms a curved backdrop for a seat overlooking the orchards.

Hitherto, I had used the area beyond the hedge to house plants with apricot and coral flowers, which are not always the easiest ones to place, whereas the Mediterranean Bank itself now had quite a collection of pink-flowered plants. With the removal of the rhododendron hedge the challenge was to unite this area as one. Initially, I decided that we should settle for a mixture of pink and orange, with a lot of blue and some

The Mediterranean Bank in May

white. However, over the last few years we have only retained those pinks which incline towards shades of peach and coral, such as *Diascia integerrima* and *D. vigilis*, *Salvia* 'Rimambelle', *S.* 'Salmon', *S.* 'Señorita Leah' and *S.* 'Trelawny Rose Pink', with a substantial amount of silver, grey and dark red foliage to offset them. Although perhaps not strictly speaking 'Mediterranean', we have increased the number of roses on this bank, where they seem to flourish, in shades of apricot and soft orange. The most recent addition has been three intersectional (Itoh hybrid) *Paeonia* 'Copper Kettle', which has mouth-wateringly beautiful flowers of coppery pink.

The season starts with tulips. First in flower is the pink and yellow species *Tulipa saxatilis*. This is followed by groups of the orange *T.* 'Request' and *T.* 'Jimmy', then a large planting of the low-growing *Iris* 'Broadleigh Rose' with its pink falls marked with yellow. After this come *Paeonia* 'Copper Kettle' and *Achillea* 'Salmon Beauty' followed by roses and salvias.

ABOVE *Rosa* 'Lady Emma Hamilton' and *Salvia* 'Purple Queen'
RIGHT (CLOCKWISE FROM TOP LEFT) *Achillea* 'Salmon Beauty' and *Lavandula* 'Munstead Blue';
Rosa 'The Lady of Shalott'; *Sedum* 'Hab Grey' and *Salvia* 'Salmon'; *Paeonia* 'Copper Kettle'

My favourite rose amongst them is 'Lady Emma Hamilton'. It has delectable apricot flowers with foliage verging on dark red and is quite exquisite. The other roses in these shades are 'Lady of Shalott', 'The Lark Ascending', 'Louise Clements', 'Meg', 'Mrs Oakley Fisher' and 'Sally Holmes', the last of which starts with apricot buds before opening to white flowers with just a hint of apricot-pink. The last and longest flowering components in this colour are the shrubby salvias mentioned above, which for the most part appear to be hardy in our garden if the winter isn't too extreme. It is hard to imagine how we managed without the wonderful range of shrubby salvias emanating from Central and South America. When we took on the garden we only had two, both red: *Salvia grahamii*, now known as *S. microphylla* var. *neurepia*, which is just hardy, and *S. confertiflora*, which is only half-hardy. And now I believe we have around fifty from purple, blue, pale blue, red, apricot, yellow, deep pink, pale pink to white and varying shades within these colours. It is a wonderful palette for gardeners to play with.

The Mediterranean Bank in June

In the early part of the season there are some whites on the bank in the form of cistus, *Libertia grandiflora* (syn. *L. chilensis*), *Anthericum liliago*, *Paeonia* 'Duchesse de Nemours', *Asphodelus albus* and *Paradisea lusitanica*. Then from June onwards, blues and purples become more prominent with several unnamed irises, *Parahebe perfoliata*, *Nepeta* 'Six Hills Giant', *Eryngium bourgatii*, *Geranium* 'Rozanne', *Lavandula* 'Hidcote' and *L*. 'Munstead', *Clematis* 'Cassandra' and *C*. × *jouiniana*, *Salvia* 'Purple Queen' and *S*. 'Javier', *Agapanthus* 'Sandringham' and *A*. 'Doctor Brouwer'. By August and September there are also a number of different sedums flowering in colours ranging from buff to copper-pink and red.

While I have included the Mediterranean Bank in order to describe the colour scheme which has evolved over more recent years, it is not a typical border; in keeping with the type of plants content to grow on sunny, stony, Mediterranean slopes, this bank probably has a greater preponderance of shrubs than most of our borders. Foliage plays an important part. There is a lot of grey and silver foliage, together with the red leaves of some roses, heucheras and sedums and the bright green of two large *Euphorbia stygiana* and other euphorbias with their yellow-green flower heads. Apart from the roses, salvias and other shrubs, two different varieties of olive adorn the top of the bank, both left behind after photo shoots, which have now grown to a considerable height. There are also two buddlejas: *B. colvilei and B. salviifolia* planted halfway down the bank. I believe the former favours being grown against a warm wall, but I was tempted to try it as a free-standing shrub on the bank. Although it grows well with good foliage, so far it has been reluctant to produce more than a few of the beautiful deep pink racemes for which it is renowned, while the latter one has lovely purple flowers in late spring, after which its foliage starts to deteriorate during the rest of summer. So they are both under review! One has to be sanguine when it comes to gardening. Not everything works and one learns best by trial and error because conditions vary so considerably. We are constantly editing, making small changes and occasionally some more substantial ones. It is this process of forever trying to improve a planting effect which keeps me on my toes and provides endless challenges and, ultimately, pleasure.

I love this bank because it is markedly different from a conventional border and you only reach it when you round the corner at the bottom of the Water Garden so it comes as something of a surprise, which I feel contributes to a visitor's experience of the garden. It is also physically the most difficult area to work in because the incline is so steep and my feet are in constant danger of slipping, possibly damaging plants. It is hard to describe when the Mediterranean Bank is at its best, probably for a while in late May and early June and again when the roses, sedums and agapanthus are flowering towards the end of August.

THE ROSE BANK AND MIDSUMMER BORDER

The yew hedge at the bottom of the main lawn below the entrance terrace was planted to celebrate my husband's birth in 1940. On the other side of the hedge, not visible from the house, is another bank which we call the Rose Bank. It is hard to recall what was there when we started gardening in 1991. I know there were a number of rugosa roses. Some have died, but we still have two of them, 'Blanc Double de Coubert' and 'Belle Poitevine', and the latter is one of the most rewarding, long-flowering scented roses in the garden with beautiful double deep pink flowers spanning most of the months from June to September. Another good rose from that period is still going strong: 'Sheelagh Baird', a charming plant whose pink flowers are streaked with white. There were two large philadelphus, lilacs and hebes, which we have removed. I quickly decided to plant more and more roses on this bank, which now number around forty, some singly and some in threes. In addition to the structure provided by the roses we have introduced *Buddleja* 'Lochinch' and *B.* crispa, four tree peonies, four Itoh hybrid peonies, two deciduous ceanothus, two specimens of *Melianthus major* and several of the tall pink *Salvia involucrata*. For herbaceous companion planting there are hardy geraniums, alliums, nepetas,

OPPOSITE The Rose Bank in June

ABOVE The Rose Bank in early July showing roses, penstemons, salvias, achilleas and nepetas

LEFT *Paeonia rockii* hybrid seedling

peonies, eryngiums, penstemons, sedums, *Anemone × hybrida*, asters and many more plants in sympathetic colours with the cast of roses from dark reds through deep to light shades of pink and white.

There is a grass path below the Rose Bank and below that is what we rather loosely call the Midsummer Border for want of a better description. This is a huge border. In the late 1960s when my father-in-law was accumulating a considerable number of wildfowl, it was decided to take in part of what had been an agricultural field below the existing garden boundary fence, which ran directly through the middle of what is now the Midsummer Border, to create an area for the ducks, geese, flamingos and cranes. I recall a few herbaceous plants on the garden side of the fence and some shrubs on the field side, now known as the Goose Park, although we got rid of the geese when we moved in. The only things remaining today from that era are the *Acer griseum* at the hedge end of the border and the *Liquidambar styraciflua* at the other end.

In the early days of running our Garden School, we had invited my father-in-law's cousin Anthony du Gard Pasley, a distinguished landscape architect, to deliver a lecture. It always amuses me to recount how when my husband went to collect him from Northampton Station,

as he emerged from the train he handed his suitcase to Ian, who then proceeded to follow behind in the role of his porter. This must have been a bizarre sight because he would have been clad in his habitual deerstalker, cape, three-piece tweed suit with watch chain and cane, for all the world looking just like Hercule Poirot. He particularly enjoyed lecturing at Coton because he claimed there were so many things that were wrong in the garden and it gave him the opportunity to show how it should not be done. He was never shy about delivering blunt advice. On his first visit round the garden the night before his talk, he pointed with his cane at the wire fence which ran through this border and said, 'Remove this wirescape.' We were a bit shaken, but he wasn't wrong. So obediently following his advice, we then attempted to try and dig up the 1.5 m/5 ft fence which went below ground to keep out rabbits and other animals in the days before the whole garden had been fenced after taking in some of the field. In

LEFT Grass path between the Rose Bank (right) and the Midsummer Border (left)
ABOVE View of the Rose Bank and the Midsummer Border in July

addition, the fence posts had been cemented in. So removing this structure took a very long time and a not inconsiderable amount of effort. Of course, he was right. Sometimes when you live with something over time you perhaps don't see it in the way that a visitor might, and we were grateful that he more or less instructed us to do it.

The reason for this preamble about the background of the Rose Bank and the Midsummer Border is that, as you stand below the Midsummer Border, the two are viewed simultaneously, and unless somebody is walking along the path that divides them, from June onwards it appears to be one vast border. Therefore, having planted roses in the hues described above on the Rose Bank and companion planting in shades of purple, blue, pink and white, it seemed natural to continue with this theme in the large border below. As I write there are also eighteen roses running through it.

The colour that probably stands out most clearly in these two areas is deep pink. There are so many roses in this colour, which to me conveys a feeling of warmth, and amongst the herbaceous planting in the Midsummer Border it is echoed in hardy geraniums, achilleas, penstemons, monardas, shrubby salvias, veronicastrum, echinaceas, phlox, lythrum and dahlias. The colour scheme here is not dissimilar to the Acacia Border, but there the deeper purple-pink is more intense and to my eye has a slightly more sombre effect. The Rose Bank is at its fullest and most colourful from mid-June to mid-July, but the Midsummer Border reaches a crescendo through August into September when so many of the later flowering herbaceous plants come into their own.

While the planting in the Midsummer Border may evoke a sense of harmony, the even larger border at the other side of the Goose Park is more about contrast. In this area we

Lower side of the Midsummer Border in September

had to undertake a similar exercise to remove the original field fence before we could think about creating a border. In the early days of gardening here, we also removed about four huge and rather ordinary conifers. Many years later an enthusiastic visitor who was an expert on trees gave us a Wellingtonia, *Sequoiadendron giganteum*, which we planted with the intention of screening the rather unattractive fence at the edge of the garden where this large border ends. So it was planted amongst some *Viburnum opulus* and above a dark red berberis hedge. More recently, since the Wellingtonia has gained considerable height, we have taken out the berberis and the rather tired specimens of viburnum, and it now stands free of the border in its own space, as such a magnificent tree deserves.

LEFT ABOVE *Echinacea purpurea*, *Aster × frikartii* 'Monch' and *Eupatorium purpureum*
LEFT BELOW *Persicaria bistorta* 'Superbum', *Iris sibirica* 'Silver Edge' (and the rusty bark of *Acer griseum*)
ABOVE View through the Midsummer Border to the Wildflower Meadow and beyond, featuring *Clematis × durandii*, *Cleome hassleriana* 'Violet Queen', *Dahlia* 'Allan Sparkes' and *Clematis viticella* 'Madame Julia Correvon'

THE RED BORDER

Originally this had been my mother-in-law's nursery bed, where she put plants that she had bought while deciding where to position them and other plants that were destined for the nursery to divide or be used for cutting material. Adjacent to it was a huge specimen of *Viburnum plicatum* var. *tomentosum*, a spectacular shrub flowering in May which spanned the distance from the edge of the canal on the top side and almost argued for space with the white mulberry tree, *Morus alba*, below the border on the bottom side. I saw this as an opportunity to house red plants, as rather like the ones in salmon colours, they can look too strident against other colour schemes. However, as so often happens in a garden, the viburnum gradually started to die off, and after a few years of tidying it up, we had to give up and remove it. By this stage I had already used the space beyond the viburnum to plant what we rather

ABOVE The Red Border with dahlias, euphorbias and penstemons
RIGHT *Penstemon* 'King George', *Monarda* 'Gardenview Scarlet', *Persicaria* 'Fat Domino', *Dahlia* 'Shooting Star' and *Echinacea* 'Green Jewel'

unimaginatively call the Blue and Yellow Border, and I felt the need to create a visual colour barrier to disguise the juxtaposition between the two areas. We therefore put in a number of plants with green and fairly neutral-coloured flowers, such as *Euphorbia wallichii*, *Scabiosa columbaria* subsp. *ochroleleuca*, *Selinum wallichianum*, *Echinacea* 'White Swan' and the tall *Bidens heterophylla* with its masses of lovely small, creamy yellow flowers, which is planted at intervals throughout the borders at the top of the Goose Park.

In selecting red flowering plants for this border, I was careful to choose those which didn't err on the side of blue or orange. Unlike traditional 'hot' schemes, I have eschewed using adjacent spectrum colours of orange and strong yellow, which I find too powerful for the context in which I am planting, or including violet-blues which are often adopted in such schemes. My own preference is for masses of green to offset the strength of the red and some pale yellow flowering plants to show the red to advantage. Over the years we have revised some of the red plants originally included. We struggled with *Lobelia* 'Queen Victoria' before giving up because the conditions in our clay soil in full sun were clearly too dry for its liking. *Hemerocallis* 'Stafford', although attractive, needs constant deadheading and its foliage deteriorates after flowering, so that went too. *Helenium* 'Moerheim Beauty' is another one we dispensed with because it needs endless deadheading in order to retain red rather than brown flowers.

It is hard to resist the beauty of oriental poppies, and *Papaver* 'Beauty of Livermere' is the first plant to flower in this bed in late May/early June. It is important to place these poppies where their post-flowering remains, which need cutting to the ground, can be disguised by something flowering later in front of their space. It is interesting how few red flowering plants perform before mid-June. *Geum* 'Mrs Bradshaw' is an invaluable contributor in this early gap and will continue to flower for weeks if deadheaded. Then we have *Achillea* 'Paprika', *Crocosmia* 'Lucifer', *Potentilla* 'Gibson's Scarlet' and *P.* 'Monsieur Rouillard', *Penstemon* 'King George', *Salvia* 'Royal Bumble', *Persicaria amplexicaulis* 'Fat Domino', *Dahlia* 'Bishop of Auckland', *D.* 'Bishop of Llandaff', *D.* 'Ragged Robin' and *D.* 'Witteman's Best'. Perhaps the most intensely red flowers in this border belong to *Rosa* 'Dublin Bay', which is usually regarded as a wall shrub or climber, but here is grown as a large free-standing shrub. It is a perfectly pure red and a repeat-flowering rose with a long season dominating the reds in this colourful border.

Euphorbia wallichii, *E. ceratocarpa* and *E. schillingii* produce vibrant yellow-green flowers over a very long period. *Nicotiana* 'Lime Green' and *Echinacea* 'Green Jewel' both have green flowers, while *E.* 'White Swan' has white flowers tinged with green and *E.* 'Jade' has green centres. There is a mass of green foliage in most of the plants already mentioned, all of which contribute to the green effect. Pale yellow comes initially with ten plantings of *Tulipa* 'Maja' throughout both parts of this border. In its correct form this tulip is a delicious pale yellow, but occasionally we have been supplied with something masquerading under this name which is a rather unattractive bright yellow. This is unfortunately a hazard that all gardeners face when ordering tulips from wholesalers. The theme is then picked up with *Lupinus* 'Chandelier', *Iris sibirica* 'White Swirl' (which has yellow markings), the pale yellow roses 'Albéric Barbier' and 'Imogen', *Nepeta govaniana*, *Kniphofia* 'Percy's Pride' and *K.* 'Bees' Lemon', *Bidens heterophylla*, *Dahlia* 'Shooting Star' in creamy yellow – a substantial dahlia which makes a big impact and is repeated along the blue and yellow section of the border beyond – and in a slightly stronger yellow there is *Achillea* 'Cloth of Gold'. This part of the bed really looks quite impressive from late June onwards and probably reaches its best moment when the dahlias are performing in August and September.

RIGHT ABOVE *Rosa* 'Dublin Bay' and *Nepeta govaniana*
RIGHT BELOW *Kniphofia* 'Percy's Pride', *Dahlia* 'Witteman's Best', *Euphorbia ceratocarpa* and *Echinacea* 'Jade'

THE BLUE AND YELLOW BORDER

I find the combination of blue or purple and yellow one of the most satisfying colour schemes – and one which frequently causes me to smile – and I would suggest that in this border there is an even balance between the two colours with neither being dominant. Once the tulips have finished flowering in May, it takes a while, perhaps until the middle of June depending on the season, for the border to come alive. Amongst the blues are *Geranium × magnificum*, well named for its brilliant blue flowers, and the quieter *G. pratense* 'Mrs Kendall Clark'. Flowering at the same time are clumps of a two-toned purple and black iris and *Lupinus* 'The Governor'. Following on are forms of herbaceous salvias, 'May Night', 'Viola Klose' and somewhat later 'Caradonna', with purple flowers. *Amsonia orientalis* (formerly known as *Rhazya orientali*s)

ABOVE The Blue and Yellow Border with *Galega* 'His Majesty' and *Rosa* 'Maigold'
RIGHT ABOVE *Lupinus* 'Chandelier', *Rosa* 'Sweet Juliet', *Rudbeckia* 'Green Wizard' and *Delphinium* 'Black Knight'
RIGHT BELOW *Campanula lactiflora*, *Amsonia orientalis*, *Salvia* 'Caradonna' and *Rosa* 'Maigold'

is a hugely valuable plant with mid-blue flowers which last for at least two months. *Baptisia australis*, with its blue pea-like flowers, is similar to amsonia in retaining good foliage after flowering which does not require cutting back. Then there are *Geranium* 'Nimbus', *Delphinium* 'Faust' and *D.* 'Black Knight', *Campanula lactiflora* 'Prichard's Variety', *Nepeta subsessilis*, the brilliant blue and scented herbaceous *Clematis heracleifolia* 'Cassandra', *Agastache* 'Blue Fortune' and *Salvia* 'Amistad'. Dark blue *Clematis* 'Black Prince' clambers up both frames with *Rosa* 'Maigold'. *Aconitum carmichaelii* 'Spätlese' and *A.* × *arendsii* are probably the last in the cast of blue flowers in this area.

Overlapping with the flowering of *Tulipa* 'Maja' are several plantings of a little-known pale yellow pea flower, *Thermopsis lanceolata*, followed by *Iris* 'Rajah', *Lupinus* 'Chandelier', *Euphorbia wallichii*, *Achillea* 'Inca Gold' and *A.* 'Moonshine', *Paeonia lutea* var. *ludlowii*, *Rosa* 'Maigold', *R.* 'Imogen' and *R.* 'Buff Beauty', *Digitalis lutea* and *D. ferruginea*, *Alstroemeria* 'Yellow Friendship', *Hemerocallis* 'Cream Drop' and *H. dumortieri*, the yellow hollyhock *Alcea rugosa*, *Primula florindae*, *Helenium* 'Sahin's Early Flowerer', *Kniphofia* 'Percy's Pride', *K.* 'Green Jade' and *K.* 'Wrexham Buttercup', *Lysimachia ciliata* 'Firecracker', *Rudbeckia*

'Goldsturm' and *R. fulgida* var. *deamii*, *Bidens heterophylla*, *Dahlia* 'Shooting Star', *D.* 'Banana Cabana', *D.* 'Café au Lait' and *D.* 'Glorie van Noordwijk'.

In terms of creating pleasing contrasts, it is hard to improve on a composition that, for example, includes the flat yellow heads of *Achillea* 'Moonshine' against the looser form of the mid-blue *Nepeta subsessilis* and the more vertical shapes of yellow *Lupinus* 'Chandelier' and violet *Salvia* × *sylvestris* 'May Night'. This huge border is full of such pictures through the months of June to September, perhaps at its most impressive in late June and again in September.

LEFT *Euphorbia wallichii*, *Geranium* × *magnificum*, *Delphinium* 'Black Knight' and *Lupinus* 'Chandelier'
ABOVE Top side of the Blue and Yellow Border showing *Verbena bonariensis*, *Rudbeckia fulgida* var. *deamii* and *Dahlia* 'Clair de Lune'

THE MEADOW BORDER

For me and I think for those who help me in the garden, this is our favourite border. It is one that we started from scratch in the early 1990s. It occurred to me that in order to make this border visible from the top of the Goose Park, we would need to use a colour that would stand out well, and therefore we opted for orange. To this we added contrasting blues and purples, but also for fun we added in splashes of deep pink to make the colour scheme more vibrant.

It starts with the elegant *Tulipa* 'Ballerina' in strong tones of orange. It was only a while after we had embarked on the planting here that I realized how perfect the choice of orange was, as it is a place where our flamingos, whose plumage can look quite orange, tend to congregate and they actually add to the effect – pure serendipity. Initially we planted some shrubs, but gradually we have removed them except for the delicate purple-flowered *Buddleja lindleyana*. So the planting is almost completely herbaceous and in that respect very different from the other large borders. As I have mentioned elsewhere, apart from choosing plants with colours that would show from a distance, I have also sought to reflect the planting in the meadow beyond with, for example, daisy flowers in echinaceas, heleniums and asters; thistles in echinops and centaureas; buttercups in geums and potentillas; yarrow in achilleas; meadow cranesbills in geraniums; and poppies and foxgloves in their garden forms. We used to have various miscanthus grasses in this border, echoing the grasses in the meadow, but reluctantly we decided to remove them because they quickly became too big and out of scale with the surrounding planting, and it required a huge effort to dig them up in order to split and replace them with a smaller group.

Early on we rely on the tall orange *Geum* 'Totally Tangerine' and slightly shorter *G.* 'Prinses Juliana' along with orange *Papaver orientale* for colour. They are shown to advantage against the blue of *Geranium* × *magnificum*, *Centaurea montana* and *Nepeta* 'Six Hills Giant'. Then there are *Potentilla russelliana* 'William Rollison' in a strong orange, *Digitalis parviflora* and *D. parviflora* 'Milk Chocolate' in muted copper tones, *Achillea* 'Inca Gold' and *A.* 'Terracotta', *Kniphofia* 'Tawny King' and yellow *K.* 'Brimstone'. The orange theme is then taken up by the strong tones of *Helenium* 'Sahin's Early Flowerer', the orange flowers of *Ligularia dentata* 'Desdemona' and the apricot *Dahlia* 'Glorie van Noordwijk' in groups of single- and double-flowered forms, a colour echoed by a self-seeding nasturtium. The strong burnt orange of the annual marigold *Tagetes* 'Cinnabar' contributes a sharp emphasis to the border, together with

RIGHT ABOVE *Ligularia dentata* 'Desdemona', *Tulipa* 'Ballerina' and flamingos
RIGHT BELOW *Dahlia* 'Glorie van Noordwijk', *Verbena bonariensis* and *Crocosmia* 'Zambesi'

Crocosmia 'Zambesi', while towards the end of the season two late flowering forms of *Kniphofia rooperi* and *K. caulescens* make bold statements with their poker-like flowers.

Lythrum salicaria and *Echinacea purpurea* 'Magnus' add deep pink into the mix, and in the case of the echinacea the hint of orange in its cones connects with surrounding orange flowers. Blues and purples are found in *Amsonia* 'Ernst Pagels' and *A. hubrichtii*, *Geranium* 'Rozanne', *Echinops bannaticus* 'Taplow Blue', *Campanula lactiflora*, *Agastache* 'Blue Fortune', *Perovskia atriplicifolia* 'Blue Spire', *Aster × frikartii* 'Jungfrau', *Aster* (syn. *Symphyotrichum*) 'Little Carlow' and *A.* (syn. *S.*) *laeve* 'Calliope', *Aconitum carmichaelii* 'Spätlese' and *A. carmichaelii* 'Kelmscott'. Undoubtedly, the most impressive moment in this border is from mid-August into October. Perhaps I should add here that after the hugely hot and dry summer of 2022, this border never managed to reach its full potential. It has no form of irrigation and is completely exposed to the sun. Despite occasional watering with a hose we were unable to counteract the effect of the extreme heat and drought, and it was a mere shadow of its normal self.

While the colours give this border its vibrancy, as an island bed the shapes are also an important feature in providing structure, particularly in the absence of shrubs. We have deliberately chosen contrasting shapes: for example, the spherical heads of the echinops, the flat heads of the achilleas, the vertical emphasis of lythrum, kniphofia, agastache and aconitum compared with the more rounded shapes of dahlias and asters and other plants. This is a theme which I will focus on further in the next chapter.

View across the Meadow Border in August

Composing and Managing Borders

I HAVE DELIBERATELY used the word 'composing' to describe how to create and manage a border because it seems to me that there is a useful analogy between the musical instruments at a composer's disposal and the plants which a gardener uses. In gardening terms, plants are the instruments, and the gardener needs to know how they perform and how to put them together for maximum effect. This metaphor can be extended to include texture, colour, timing, rhythm, repetition, mood and, if you like, movements/seasons.

There are basic facts which will dictate to some extent what is appropriate for a border in a particular place. Perhaps the first consideration is the orientation of the space: whether it is in full sun or partial shade; the background – a hedge, a wall or maybe it is an island bed; the soil – clay, sand, chalk or loam (if you are very lucky); and the pH – alkaline or acid. All of these factors will influence the choice of plants.

Invariably you find yourself dealing with a space that already has some planting, and you need to consider whether to retain some of the existing plants, whether to rearrange them and remove some, or whether to start with a completely blank canvas and remove everything. You also need to decide whether to have a mixed border with some shrubs or entirely perennials. If the planting area is in view of the house, it probably makes sense to include a few shrubs so that there will be some structure and possibly some winter interest. Most of

Red and Midsummer Borders in September

the borders in our garden do include shrubs, perhaps more in the form of roses and what I would describe as subshrubs like euphorbias, salvias and deciduous ceanothus. The problem with shrubs in a border is that over the years they can get too large and overshadow other planting, and they tend to have only a shortish flowering season. At least roses and shrubs flowering on the current year's wood, both of which should be pruned in spring, can to some extent be contained.

Soil improvement is probably one of the first considerations, unless it is already in good condition. When we start a new border from what had been a grassed area, after removing the turf we like to cover the area in a thick layer of cow manure and leave it to rot down over the winter. Frost will help to break down the muck, and then it will greatly improve the digging potential in the spring. However, invariably there isn't time to undertake this procedure, in which case we introduce a mixture of our own well-rotted compost from garden waste, leaf mould, maybe some gritty burnt soil from underneath the bonfire to improve our clay and, if necessary, some gravel to improve the drainage. Even when we are replanting an area within a border, we will add a combination of garden compost and leaf mould to improve the texture of the soil before putting in a new group of plants.

Structure may be next on the list to consider because, if it is thought about carefully, it will produce a more interesting and satisfying end result. It is common to place all the taller plants at the back, graduating to the smallest ones at the front. To me that is totally unsatisfying. I like to stagger taller plantings (such as large euphorbias and shrub roses) with some near the front. This creates an opportunity to look through the border at angles, thereby adding an extra dimension to what otherwise is only observed from the front and maybe the ends. There are so many features that provide structure. It could start with the wall or hedge backing the area. Structures for supporting climbing roses and clematis give a sense of height and interest. Many plants in a group can make a statement due to their height. There needs to be an interplay juxtaposing tall, medium and short plants. It is important to vary foliage shapes and flower head shapes. So, for example, if one takes plants with spire-like flower heads such as delphinium, aconitum and veronicastrum, and this pattern of spires is repeated at intervals, it is more restful for the eye and creates a sense of rhythm. It is particularly effective to use repetition amongst the plants along the frontage.

Colour was covered in the previous chapter, but it is worth thinking about what colours might be used at an early stage in planning a border. You may want to pick up and run with the

RIGHT ABOVE The Rose Bank showing structure provided by roses and tree peonies
RIGHT BELOW Repetition of reds and blues in the Holly Hedge Border

colours of existing plants or select colours that would look effective against a wall or hedge. The amount of shade or sun may suggest brighter or softer colours. Whatever you choose, I find it is worth limiting and repeating them for a pleasing effect.

Plant selection will obviously depend on the scale of the border, but it is worth bearing in mind the mantra 'less is more'. In other words, even in a small area a few larger plantings, perhaps mixed with the odd smaller groups, will work better than a mass of small ones. In the early days of gardening at Coton, my husband's distinguished garden designer cousin, Anthony du Gard Pasley, told him that my planting was 'too fussy'. That stung, but it did check me and made me reassess my thinking. I tend to plant in odd numbers – threes, fives, sevens and nines – and where appropriate may use a single planting of something reasonably tall, like *Althaea cannabina* or *Salvia* 'Amistad', which will probably be repeated where there is enough space to do so.

Given the variety of fresh green foliage in spring and early summer, I would suggest that there is less necessity for so much flower colour in the early part of the season. On the whole, plants flowering before the end of June will tend to last for two to three weeks, while those flowering from July onwards are more likely to go on for six to twelve weeks or more. So I find it is worthwhile to plant one-third of the border with those that flower early like aquilegias, poppies, lupins, alliums, nepeta, iris and peonies and to leave two-thirds for later performers. Some early flowering plants such as pulmonaria, hardy geranium, nepeta, brunnera, centaurea, alchemilla, herbaceous salvia and even delphinium will flower again if they are cut back hard to the ground after flowering, including the foliage. Other plants, like oriental poppies and hemerocallis, may not flower again after being cut back but should produce fresh foliage – an improvement on yellowing leaves.

Once decisions have been made about positioning of structural plants such as roses, shrubs, tall perennials and subshrubs, thought needs to be given to other perennials, annuals, biennials, half-hardy plants and bulbs. The challenge with perennials is to achieve continuity of flowering. It takes time to learn when particular plants flower and for how long they will perform, and this will also be affected by the weather. Two perennials in our garden which probably flower over the longest period are *Aster × frikartii* 'Monch' and *Helenium* 'Sahin's Early Flowerer' – usually from July until November. The other mainstays are dahlias and shrubby salvias, which again will probably flower for about the same length of time. However,

RIGHT (CLOCKWISE FROM TOP LEFT) *Aster × frikartii* 'Monch'; *Monarda* 'Gardenview Scarlet'; *Helenium* 'Sahin's Early Flowerer'; *Achillea* 'Inca Gold'

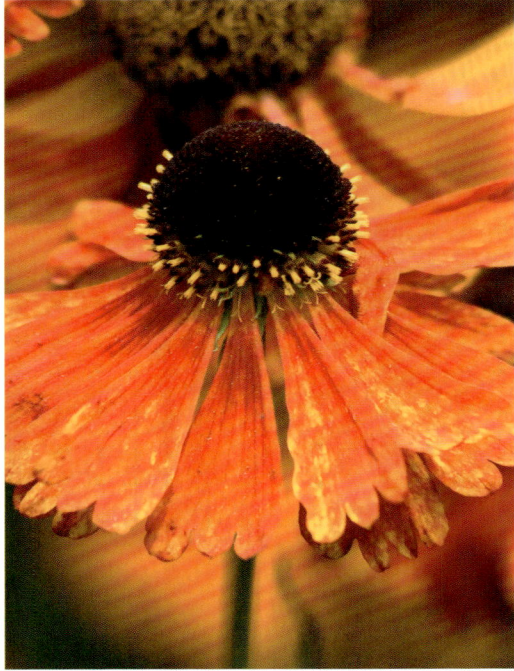

there are so many perennials that will perform for six or more weeks and it is impossible to name them all here. It may help to consult the section on 'Plants: Friends and Foes' to see which ones I favour and the lists of border plants at the end of this book.

When selecting perennials for a border I will tend to limit and repeat them as I do with colours. In this way it is easier to define the character of different areas, and similarly limiting and repeating shapes is easier on the eye. There are certain families of plants which have different species and varieties that perform through the season, such as campanula, thalictrum and aconitum. All three groups have forms flowering from spring through to autumn. In most cases the foliage is recognisably similar, which lends a sense of unity. Then there are groups of perennials – such as persicaria, astilbe, phlox, monarda, achillea, helenium, veronicastrum, herbaceous salvia, alstroemeria, *Anemone × hybrida* and aster – which appear in differing shades and colours with only slightly different timings. Most perennials will look better and flower for longer if regularly deadheaded. This is particularly true of achillea, campanula, knautia, monarda, phlox and helenium. If you have time this is quite a therapeutic pastime and is particularly rewarding when you see the results of your effort.

Bulbs can be a problem in borders and need to be placed carefully. Generally speaking, I avoid putting daffodils in borders, the exception being *N*. 'Jenny', a delicate pale lemon narcissus, which I have planted in groups at intervals along the back of the very long Holly Hedge Border to create just a little bit of interest before the tulips flower. There it looks good against the dark green glittery leaves of the holly. Elsewhere, narcissus are planted in the Woodland, Water and Bog Gardens, the orchards and other marginal areas. So the first serious planting of bulbs in borders is tulips. I will usually put in up to ten groups, depending on the border's size. They will be groups of single colours varying from place to place. We dig up the tulips once they have finished flowering and then use the space for dahlias, half-hardy salvias or annuals. After, and sometimes overlapping with, tulips are alliums. In May and June we have *A*. 'Purple Sensation', *A. nigrum* and *A. cristophii*, and on the Rose Bank in July the later flowering *A. sphaerocephalon*. There are a few lilies in one or two places and in the Holly Hedge Border in July the delightful *Galtonia candicans* – like an elegant giant snowdrop – planted at intervals along the front. Later in the season we use the beautiful scented Abyssinian gladiolus, *Acidanthera bicolor*, on the terraces round the house and in some of the Rose Garden beds.

RIGHT ABOVE *Allium* 'Purple Sensation' with wisteria in the background, which sadly died in 2022
RIGHT BELOW *Acidanthera bicolor* in September

Probably the most colourful and valuable plants for the latter part of the summer season are dahlias and shrubby salvias. It is well worth allowing plenty of space for both these groups to keep the borders looking good into early autumn. We leave nearly all our salvias in over the winter and most survive unless it is very cold, which it has seldom been in recent years. There are one or two we lift because they are less reliable and we may need the space for tulips. With the dahlias we lift all except the species ones – *D. merckii* and *D. sherffii* – which seem to get through the winter whatever the weather is like. We mainly lift the other dahlias because we need the space for tulips and because we will need to divide some in the spring for selling.

Annuals are invaluable for summer flowering. They have the advantage of performing for a long time and even longer when deadheaded. In various beds we have the enchanting

ABOVE *Salvia involucrata, Phlox* × arendsii 'Luc's Lilac' and *Actaea cimicifuga* var. *racemosa*
RIGHT (CLOCKWISE FROM TOP LEFT) *Dahlia* 'Bishop of Llandaff'; *D.* 'Labyrinth'; *D.* 'Geri Hoek'; *D.* 'Shooting Star'

ABOVE (CLOCKWISE FROM TOP LEFT) *Omphalodes linifolia*; *Nicotiana mutabilis* 'Marshmallow'; *Orlaya grandiflora*; *Hibiscus trionum*
LEFT *Cleome hassleriana* 'Cherry Queen'
RIGHT *Lunaria annua* (left); *Digitalis purpurea* (right)

Omphalodes linifolia, a small white flower resembling broderie anglaise, in early summer, and also the delicate love-in-a-mist, *Nigella damascena*. In the Rose Garden beds we plant the pretty white *Orlaya grandiflora*, which is like a refined form of cow parsley. This replaces some of the tulips and will perform from late May into July, when we put in *Acidanthera bicolor*, as mentioned above. In other tulip spots in this area we plant the dark red *Antirrhinum* 'Black Prince' and a strong pink cleome called 'Cherry Queen'. In the Holly Hedge Border we plant an unusual annual called *Hibiscus trionum*, which we are constantly being asked to identify. Flowering later in this border is the tall white *Nicotiana sylvestris*. On the Mediterranean and Rose Banks we often plant the unusual glaucous annual with purple flowers, *Cerinthe major* 'Purpurascens'. The Rose Bank also has several groups of *Antirrhinum* 'Black Prince' and *A. majus* 'Admiral White' plus the white form of cleome. In both the Acacia Border and the Midsummer Border we use *Nicotiana mutabilis* 'Marshmallow' and the purple *Cleome* 'Violet Queen'. The Red Border has *Nicotiana* 'Lime Green', and the Meadow Border includes groups of the marigold *Tagetes* 'Cinnabar' in strong orange with hints of dark red.

My favourite biennials are honesty, *Lunaria annua*, flowering in May; foxgloves, *Digitalis purpurea*, which tend to flower through June; and *Eryngium giganteum*, known as Miss

Willmott's Ghost due to her reputed habit of dropping its seed in other people's gardens whether they wanted it or not (usually in flower in July). I particularly love both honesty and foxgloves because they lend a sense of naturalness to a border and they are easy to manage.

It is important to consider what I would describe as frontage planting. Where the front is particularly prominent, it is good practice to repeat plants there. If it is a sunny bed, irises are particularly effective as their linear foliage makes quite a statement. It is challenging to find lowish growing plants that are not going to need cutting back at some stage, which can create rather obvious gaps. Sedums are a good choice for this situation. From the moment they leaf up in spring until they come into flower in late summer and early autumn, they look attractive, especially those with smoky or red foliage, but it is important to divide the taller cultivars regularly to avoid their habit of splitting when flowering. One or two of the hardy geraniums are also useful in this respect. Forms of *G. × riversleaianum*, 'Mavis Simpson' and 'Russell Prichard', are fairly reliably continuous flowering if tidied up now and then; those of *G. sanguineum* – *G. sanguineum* var. *striatum*, 'Elke' and 'Glenluce' – just need occasional deadheading. Penstemons are invaluable too. They come in a wonderful range of colours and make a statement as a group. On the whole they will keep going if deadheaded regularly, but if the weather is hot for long periods they may need cutting right back as the foliage can start to yellow. Diascias, dianthus and nepetas will all work well for a while, but will invariably need cutting back at some stage of the summer.

Another component of border planting which it is important not to forget is foliage. There are so many facets to leaves in terms of size, shape, colour, variegation, texture, light absorbency and reflectiveness. All these finer details, if taken into consideration, can contribute to the overall design. Foliage colour is perhaps the most obvious feature. I would suggest that apart from green in any one scheme, one should limit the other colours and either use greys and silvers with perhaps a splash of bronze or red here and there, or if using variegated leaves just set them off against greens. Yellow leaves need to be used judiciously. In one bed we have two groups of *Hakonechloa macra* 'Aureola' with *Choisya ternata* 'Sundance' and some yellow poppies. Yellow foliage does need to connect with other yellows and be contrasted with lots of green to work well. Obviously, the size and shape of leaves vary considerably, and it is always worth considering when placing plants how adjacent leaves will look. You do not want plants with small, busy leaves next to each other.

RIGHT ABOVE Border with *Sedum* (*Hylotelephium*) *spectabile* as a frontage planting
RIGHT BELOW The large silver leaves of cardoon (*Cynara cardunculus*) and the dark red divided foliage of *Cimicifuga racemosa* 'Atropurpureum' adding interest amongst the surrounding greens

Leaf sizes need to be varied in planting schemes, and features like ribbed, reflective and linear leaves should be included thoughtfully to create extra interest.

In an ideal world when we are organised, we deal with staking and supporting those plants that need it in March and April. At this time of year plants grow phenomenally fast, and it is important to install supports early rather than leave the job until they have collapsed on the ground. We will have already supported those roses that require it in early spring with hazel uprights and woven rings of willow, and in some cases on metal obelisks. One of the obelisks we use is my mother-in-law's old Aga pot holder, which works well to support a viticella clematis and a perennial sweet pea. Initially, we need to stake different forms of semi-herbaceous clematis, such as *C. recta*, *C. integrifolia*, *C.* 'Petit Faucon', *C.* 'Arabella' and *C.* × *durandii*, all of which seem to require slightly different levels and types of support. For this job we use hazel branches which we interweave and, if we have to, tie in with brown flexible tie. These are also done in a pyramidical form. In April we will place hazel branches round groups of delphiniums, bending them to create a beehive to grow through. And we have to repeat this process for some groups of aconitum, notably *A.* 'Spark's Variety', and later cultivars of tall growing asters. We usually plant

OPPOSITE Structural supports
for roses and clematis made
with hazel uprights and bands
of woven willow in the Acacia
Border in early April

ABOVE Early July in the Acacia
Border, by which time the
supports are barely visible

LEFT Semi-herbaceous *Clematis
integrifolia* also supported with
hazel and willow

dahlias out towards the end of May, and then we place circular metal grow-through frames over them. Some dahlias grow so big that it requires two or three frames to hold them in place, and we have a lot of them growing in the garden, so this is a massive and time-consuming job but essential if these plants are to be shown to their best advantage.

I would also like to mention the importance of screening. There are a number of mostly early flowering perennials, such as oriental poppies, alliums, lupins, aquilegias, verbascums and peonies, which may need to be disguised after they have either finished flowering or been cut down to perform again. So it is worth thinking about planting them behind either something tall which flowers later, such as dahlias or tall shrubby salvias, or a shrub which has been cut back in spring and will grow and flower later in the season, like melianthus, buddleja and the deciduous form of ceanothus.

A border doesn't stand still. Plants increase in size and need to be reduced. They can die or lose their appeal, and places need to be found for new plants. As a gardener I am always looking for ways to improve plantings. So in August and September we start making notes about changes that we plan to undertake during the winter months. We call it 'editing'. It is

so worthwhile because memory isn't reliable enough to recall all the good ideas that we had several months earlier, and we are often surprised when reading our notes to come across plans that had been totally forgotten. Once the garden has closed at the end of September, we spend the month of October putting into place any major changes while it is still possible to see the space in relation to surrounding planting, and the height, spread and colour of adjacent plants. When things have died down in the border, it is easy to lose one's sense of geography and forget the behaviour of plants which have shrunk to ground level. The more minor changes are dealt with as and when we come to work on the border during the winter and early spring months.

LEFT Metal supports for roses and clematis in the Blue and Yellow Border
ABOVE Tall plants such as dahlias, eupatorium, phlox, Japanese anemones and vernonia disguise earlier flowering hardy geraniums and lupins which have gone over and been cut back

Smaller Beds in Shade and Sun

WHILE THE LARGE BORDERS in the garden tend to enjoy sunny conditions, there are a number of smaller beds, some of which are in shade. I enjoy the challenge of finding plants that will tolerate a shady site, and I think plantings in shade add to the character of a garden by their simplicity and understatedness. As I have already mentioned, I think it is important to keep the mantra 'less is more' in your head when thinking about a small space – in other words, a few large groups of plants, perhaps interspersed with some smaller ones, rather than a mass of small plantings which can result in a 'dolly mixture' effect.

THE STATUE BED

Backing on to the Woodland Garden is a small bed bracketed by a yew hedge. It is known as the Statue Bed because the centrepiece is a sculpture of Pan playing his pipes. The dimensions of this bed are roughly 6 m/20 ft × 1.8 m/6 ft, and it is shaded by both a tulip tree (*Liriodendron tulipifera*) and a copper beech (*Fagus sylvatica* f. *purpurea*), though it gets some sun towards the end of the afternoon. At the end of 2022 we decided that this bed needed a rethink. There seemed to be too many small plantings, and as the soil hadn't been improved for a long time, some plants were struggling, particularly as a result of the very dry summer; the sculpture of Pan also appeared out of scale with the height of the hedge.

The Dells, a quiet area for plants that enjoy dappled shade, highlighting the use of foliage plants

After all the plants had been removed, Pan and the extremely heavy base on which he was perched were lifted with considerable effort. The topsoil was removed to a sheet and 45 cm/18 inches of subsoil removed altogether. The hedge was then trimmed back quite hard. The topsoil was mixed with garden compost and put back into the bed. Meanwhile, Pan had to be detached from his circular base (which had been concealed under the soil), and a new concrete base was put in position, on to which an old piece of mossy stone was placed. A hole had to be drilled through this stone so that he could rest on it with one hoof. This elevated him to a higher position more in scale with the hedge, and he now looks as though he has just alighted and could move on at any moment.

We then set about replanting, concentrating particularly on foliage, including some silver- and grey-leafed plants, filigree ferns and linear foliage; we included more shrubs and fewer herbaceous plants than before. Apart from the ferns and a tall *Disporum cantoniense*

The Statue Bed in early July

'Green Giant', which has small green flowers, all the plants have white flowers which show up well in the shade and against the dark green background of the yew hedge. Flowering commences with hellebores, followed by leucojums – known as snowflakes – then there are the white flowers of *Brunnera macrophylla* 'Mister Morse', tulips, libertia, *Anaphalis triplinervis* 'Summer Snow', *Choisya* 'Snow Flurries', *Lilium longiflorum* 'White Heaven', *Hosta sieboldiana* var. *elegans*, *Hydrangea paniculata* 'Phantom' and *H. paniculata* 'Unique', *Persicaria amplexicaulis* 'Alba' and *Anemone* × *hybrida* 'Whirlwind'. We are hoping that they will keep a succession of flowers going through the spring and summer.

THE DELLS

There is an area below the Old Orchards which we call the Dells. In the 1980s my father-in-law deployed water that flowed underground from these orchards to create three small pools and a connecting stream running through it. My mother-in-law then designed and planted three small beds alongside the pools and stream, where she selected plants with good foliage which could cope with both damp and dry shade. The background is a lime hedge (*Tilia platyphyllos*) with large shrubs at intervals, including philadelphus, *Staphylea colchica* and *Prunus laurocerasus* 'Otto Luyken', and it is overhung by a tall lime tree (also *T. platyphyllos*), so the back part of the beds is very dry and shady, while in heavy rain the stream can flood the front edges.

In the damper areas edging the stream there are varieties of caltha, primula, hosta, rodgersia, astilbe and carex, all of which have interesting and varied foliage. There is a separate planting on the grass side of the stream which starts off with *Caltha palustris* var. 'Alba' interplanted with *Primula japonica* 'Alba'. The caltha flowers from March until the end of April, when we cut it back, and then the primula takes over through May into June, while by July the caltha flowers again. In the drier parts are *Polygonatum* × *hybridum*, *Phyllitis scolopendrium*, *Dryopteris filix-mas* 'Crispa Cristata', *Aruncus dioicus*, *Aster divaricatus* (syn. *Eurybia divaricata*), *Lythrum salicaria*, *Persicaria amplexicaulis* 'Alba', *Kirengeshoma koreana* and *Eupatorium rugosum* (syn. *Ageratum altissimum*). All of these plants are valuable for their foliage, and the ones that flower do so for long periods so are useful in small beds. Intermediate height shrubs also providing good foliage are *Sarcococca ruscifolia*, *Ribes sanguineum* 'White Icicle', *Stephanandra tanakae* with its graceful arching habit, *Hydrangea paniculata* 'Limelight' and *Ilex aquifolium* 'Ferox Argentea'.

In spring and early summer white is predominant with narcissus, *Anemone blanda* 'White Splendour', hellebores, leucojum, *Caltha palustris* var. 'Alba', *Primula japonica* 'Alba', *Ribes sanguineum* 'White Icicle', *Prunus laurocerasus* 'Otto Luyken' and the delicately scented flowers of *Staphylea colchica*. *Caltha palustris*, *Ribes odoratum*, *Primula bulleyana* and *Hemerocallis* 'Golden Chimes' add splashes of yellow. Later on, astilbe and lythrum provide shades of deep pink. I have deliberately given more space in these small beds to those plants flowering from July onwards, such as *Primula florindae*, persicaria, rodgersia, kirengeshoma, *Aster divaricatus*, lythrum, astilbe and eupatorium, as most of them will continue to flower until the end of summer.

Over the period that we have been running the garden, we have augmented the planting in the Dells with shrubs in the grass around this area to create a greater sense of depth to the rather narrow beds and to add interest to this shady part of the garden. They include two of my very favourite specimens – *Cercidiphyllum japonicum*, the katsura tree with its elegant habit, beautiful foliage, aroma of caramel in late summer and lovely autumn colour – and the exquisite *Cornus* 'Eddie's White Wonder' with elegant white flower bracts in May, a really glorious sight to behold, and red foliage in autumn. Other shrubs include *Ribes odoratum* with scented yellow flowers, *Viburnum × burkwoodii*, *Sambucus nigra* 'Guincho Purple' and *Hydrangea arborescens* 'Incrediball' – the last is like *H.* 'Annabelle' on steroids. I find this area very restful. The colours are muted but there is always something to enjoy, and it is probably one of the less demanding parts of the garden to look after.

RIGHT In the Dells, *Astilbe chinensis* var. *taquettii* 'Purpurlanze'
OPPOSITE (CLOCKWISE FROM TOP LEFT) *Primula japonica* 'Alba'; *Cornus* 'Eddie's White Wonder'; *Gillenia trifoliata*; *Hydrangea arborescens* 'Incrediball'

THE ITALIAN GARDEN

The Italian Garden, so named because of the Italian stone wellhead situated there, lies below the Acacia Border at the bottom of the main lawn under the shade of a huge horse chestnut (*Aesculus hippocastanum*). This is another area where I have selected white flowering plants with the backdrop of the dark green yew hedge and the shade created by the tree. About twenty years ago we planted three specimens of *Hydrangea* 'Annabelle' immediately under the tree, since when they have suckered and spread to the extent that we have to reduce them each year, but they do make the most wonderful picture and light up this very shady area. Quite apart from the mystery as to how the moisture-loving hydrangeas flourish among the roots of this vast tree is the magical display of snowdrops which appear in early spring through their cut-back branches.

ABOVE The Italian Garden with *Pelargonium* 'Rose Silver Cascade' planted in the lead pot in the foreground
RIGHT ABOVE Snowdrops in February growing through hydrangeas with *Helleborus foetidus* in the background
RIGHT BELOW The Italian wellhead with *Hydrangea* 'Annabelle' in the background and pots of *Argyranthemum foeniculaceum* in the foreground

In the small bed to the left of the hydrangeas which is backed by the yew hedge we have the white flowering *Rosa* 'Moonlight' (a Pemberton musk rose) and the shorter white *R.* 'Yvonne Rabier', both seemingly able to cope with the conditions of dry shade. The only other shrub is the winter-scented *Sarcococca hookeriana* var. *digyna*. White hellebores appear after the snowdrops, and they are followed by the tall white flowers of *Leucojum aestivum* 'Gravetye Giant', which flowers for a considerable length of time for an early bulb. By April, at the front edge emerge the very delicate fronds of the maidenhair fern, *Adiantum venustum*, and the pale mauve flowers of *Epimedium* 'Kaguyahime'. Next to come in May are the white flowers of the strappy leaf *Libertia grandiflora* (syn. *L. chilensis*), followed by the roses which repeat flower, and finally the white flowers of *Aster divaricatus* (syn. *Eurybia divaricata*), which go on to the end of summer.

In the wellhead we have a planting of *Hosta* 'Devon Green', and around its base in summer there are pots of heliotrope and white ivy leaf pelargoniums. The only splash of strong colour comes from the strong pink flowers of *Pelargonium* 'Rose Silver Cascade', which we plant every year in the two lead pots at either side of the frontage of this area. It is a remarkably good ivy leaf form which I inherited from my mother-in-law and seems to perform equally well in sun or shade.

THE ENTRANCE YARD

In our entrance yard there is a curved stone wall at the bottom of which is a very shallow bed facing north. It is planted with mixed colours of *Helleborus* × *hybridus* which flower in early spring, followed by new foliage which remains looking good through the rest of summer. In addition, there are a number of roses and clematis on the wall. The roses which don't seem to mind the north-facing position are pale pink 'New Dawn', white 'The Garland', dark red 'Erotica' and deep pink 'Zépherine Drouhin'. And the clematis are 'Perle d'Azur', 'Pamela', 'Black Prince' and 'Mienie Belle'. This seems to be an easy solution for a narrow north-facing bed. Also in the yard there is a small bed under the shade of a Norway maple (*Acer platanoides*), which suckers badly, backed by a laurel hedge (*Prunus laurocerasus*), so it is a fairly inhospitable place for growing plants. However, we have managed to establish a carpet of *Epimedium* × *versicolor* 'Sulphureum', which somehow seems to flourish with its pale yellow flowers in spring, followed by delicate foliage, and looks pretty amongst the suckering roots of the tree.

RIGHT ABOVE *Clematis* 'Perle d'Azur' growing through *Rosa* 'Erotica' on the wall in the lower part of the entrance yard
RIGHT BELOW *Rosa* 'Zépherine Drouhin' on the curved wall, with hellebores in the narrow bed below

THE POOP DECK BEDS

My father-in-law was an ex-naval commander who liked to give naval names to various parts of the garden, such as the semi-circular paved area with steps leading down towards the main pond he called the Poop Deck; hence the two beds beside the steps are known as the Poop Deck Beds. These small beds face due south and are in full sun for most of the day. The planting is not the same on each side of the steps, although the colours are in similar shades of deep pink, purple, blue and white. Both walls support clematis and roses. Here I find I am able to grow *Dictamnus albus* var. *purpureus*, which I have struggled with elsewhere. Another plant that enjoys the sunshine here is *Geranium palmatum*, which seems to be hardy in this situation and seeds itself readily. The deep pink of the geranium and the lilac-pink of the dictamnus are picked up by the ground-covering *Geranium sanguineum* 'Glenluce', *Rosa* 'De Rescht', *Dahlia* 'Fascination' and *Lythrum salicaria* 'Lady Sackville'; blue and purple

ABOVE *Lilium regale*, *Heuchera* 'Plum Pudding', *Lythrum salicaria* 'Lady Sackville' and *Nigella damascena* growing in the left-hand Poop Deck Bed

RIGHT *Lilium regale*, *Campanula lactiflora*, *Penstemon* 'Alice Hindley' and *Rosa* 'Little White Pet' in the right-hand Poop Deck Bed

are represented by annual nigella, *Geranium wlassovianum*, *Penstemon* 'Alice Hindley' and *P.* 'Mother of Pearl', *Campanula lactiflora*, *Clematis viticella* 'Polish Spirit', *Salvia* 'Amistad' and *S.* 'Javier', and agapanthus; while white is seen in *Rosa* 'Little White Pet', *R.* 'The Lady Scarman' and *R.* 'Prosperity', *Lilium regale*, *Hebe salicifolia* 'Spender's Seedling', *Clematis* 'Roko-Kolla', *Veronicastrum virginicum* 'Album' and an enchanting little known annual, *Hibiscus trionum*.

THE MORNING ROOM BED

The entrance to the garden brings the visitor on to the south-west terrace. Here there is a very narrow bed underneath the window of our Morning Room, so this is known as the Morning Room Bed. It is in full sun from mid-morning onwards. It is probably typical in size to many beds at the front of a house, measuring 6 m/20 ft × 0.6 m/2 ft, which can be a challenge to plant. Adorning the walls either side and underneath the window is what my mother-in-law called the 'Coton Rose', and we think these roses may even pre-date her parents' purchase of the house in the 1920s. I believe its proper name is *Rosa multiflora* 'Platyphylla' (syn. *R. multiflora* 'Grevillei' or Seven Sisters' rose). This is a beautiful once-flowering rose which opens a deep magenta-pink, fading through different shades to a pale lilac-pink. It is sweetly scented and looks charming against the honey-coloured stone of the house. On one side of the window there is *Clematis viticella* 'Odoriba' and on the other, *C. viticella* 'Madame Julia Correvon', both in similar shades to the rose. In the narrow bed underneath the window the season starts with a lovely purple fringed tulip called 'Gorilla'. Also flowering at this point are two groups of the perennial wallflower, *Erysimum* 'Bowles's Mauve'. These purple and mauve flowers are set off by the silver filigree foliage of *Artemisia nutans*, *A. alba* 'Canescens' and *Senecio viravira* and the dark red leaves of *Heuchera* 'Obsidian'. *Libertia grandiflora* (syn. *L. chilensis*) and *Allium cristophii* are next to flower, followed by *Penstemon* 'Raven' and *Salvia* 'Lalarsha'. *Dahlia* 'Purple Gem' takes the place occupied earlier by the tulips. Provided the ladder-like growths of the erysimum flowers are deadheaded from time to time, this bed will continue to retain its colour until the end of the season with very few component parts. Planted just round the corner edge of the bed is *Rosa* 'Mermaid', whose pale yellow flowers open just as 'Seven Sisters' is fading. This rose is trained higher up and continues flowering above the earlier rose into September.

One of the ways to make the most of smaller spaces is to grow something early that is summer dormant through a planting that will perform later. There are a number of examples in the garden where this works well. In one place we have an early standard pale yellow narcissus which grows through *Hosta* 'Thomas Hogg'. When the narcissus is flowering in early March there is no sign of the hosta, but as the hostas start to leaf up, they gradually rise above the fading leaves of the narcissus and neither plant seems to disturb the growth of the other. In another instance *Anemone blanda* 'White Splendour' is growing happily through *Lythrum salicaria*. The anemone flowers for a long time before it starts to fade and disappear in the spring, but the lythrum is late to emerge, so this is another pairing that seems to work well. In the Bog Garden there is a large expanse of the bright yellow *Erythronium tuolumnense* which is planted through a group of *Filipendula rubra* and a large planting of *Persicaria polymorpha*. The erythronium provides interest early on when neither of the later plants are showing, and only as it starts to fade will the filipendula and persicaria show signs of producing shoots. There are a number of early flowering plants which are summer dormant, such as forms of *Anemone blanda*, *A. nemorosa*, chionodoxa, erythronium, muscari, narcissus and, of course, snowdrop (galanthus), so it is worth considering getting double value out of an area, whether or not you are confined for space.

RIGHT (CLOCKWISE FROM TOP LEFT) *Erysimum* 'Bowles's Mauve' and *Tulipa* 'Gorilla' in the Morning Room Bed in April; *Rosa multiflora* 'Platyphylla' (Seven Sisters' rose) and *Clematis viticella* 'Madame Julia Correvon'; the Morning Room Bed in June; *Dahlia* 'Purple Gem' and *Salvia* 'Lalarsha' in late summer; *Allium christophii*

The Woodland Garden

ON A HOT DAY IN SUMMER when you walk through the arch in the Rose Garden leading to the Woodland Garden it is wonderfully cooling – the temperature seems to drop by several degrees and the mood alters dramatically. It is a glade of mature deciduous trees, with a beautiful specimen of both a tulip tree, *Liriodendron tulipifera*, and a copper beech, *Fagus sylvatica* f. *purpurea*, and a gate in the distance over which visitors can enjoy a view across a meadow to the reservoir below the garden. There is no particular colour theme in this area, and once the season moves beyond the yellow, white and purple of winter aconites (eranthis), snowdrops (galanthus), crocus and narcissus, the colours are quite muted and the general impression is of green grass and foliage with splashes of pink, white, blue, mauve and some pale yellow. In the late 1990s we removed the boundary fence and extended the Woodland Garden. My father-in-law had fenced it to protect his wildfowl from predators, and in doing so he had excluded an area of naturalised snowdrops. So we rearranged the fence to recover this part of the garden, planted a native hedge to disguise the fence and reorientated the gate to take in the view of the reservoir. This allowed us to create a path through the woodland, giving visitors a circular walk around the planted areas. It also gave me the opportunity to create three rather different types of woodland planting. Situated to the right of the gate under the copper beech there was already a bed of special spring plants, including trillium, erythronium, varieties of *Anemone nemorosa*, epimedium, cardamine and hacquetia, which are at their best in April. Many of these flowers are summer dormant, so from May onwards this part becomes quieter and relies on the different greens and foliage of various ferns, epimediums and shrubby sarcococcas, interspersed with foxgloves (*Digitalis purpurea*) and later the flowers of hydrangeas.

In the huge bed to the left of the gate, herbaceous woodlanders continue flowering quietly through the rest of the season. These plants can cope with deciduous shade and amongst them are stalwarts such as pulmonarias, the pink-flowered cow parsley (*Chaerophyllum hirsutum* 'Roseum'), the spring-flowering pea (*Lathyrus vernus*), dicentras, early aconitums, hardy geraniums, campanulas, hostas and, as summer progresses, *Aster divaricatus* (syn. *Eurybia*

RIGHT ABOVE View of the house from the Woodland Garden
RIGHT BELOW Snowdrops (*Galanthus nivalis*) in the Woodland Garden in February

divaricata), forms of *Anemone × hybrida*, *Kirengeshoma koreana*, colchicums and *Crocus speciosus* 'Oxonian'. Structure is provided by hydrangea, choisya, magnolia, sambucus and the linear foliage of clumps of *Iris foetidissima* and *Libertia grandiflora* (syn. *L. chilensis*). The longest performing plants amongst these are probably the deep pink flowers of *Geranium oxonianum* 'Claridge Druce', *G. nodosum*, *G.* 'Anne Thomson' and *G. palustre*. And the continuity of this colour, together with the delicate and intricate fronds of groups of polystichum ferns, gives a sense of coherence to the planting in this huge bed.

As you take the path through the woodland, you reach the part which is given over to naturalised planting, starting with winter aconites, then snowdrops, primroses, violets, bluebells (*Hyacinthoides non-scripta*) and their white forms (not scillas I hasten to add) and finally martagon lilies (*Lilium martagon*). The backdrop to this area is holly (ilex), and there are witch hazel (hamamelis), daphne, ribes, viburnum, philadelphus and euonymus amongst other shrubs to provide interest following the earlier performance of bulbs.

So many people find it difficult to deal with planting in shade. It is obviously important to select species which can cope with dry conditions and the competition of tree roots, but

it can also be immensely satisfying. It is more relaxed and fun to play with the contrasting textures of foliage. It is a good idea to include some plants with light-reflective leaves, such as mahonia, holly, fatshedera and choisya, as a contrast to the light absorbency of most woodland plant foliage. One thing I only discovered fairly recently is the effectiveness of using *Ribes sanguineum* 'White Icicle' in shady areas in early spring. It is the most beautiful and graceful shrub with racemes of white flowers which highlight these areas, and I now have ten of them throughout the shadier parts of the garden, three in the woodland area.

However, I should perhaps add here that many woodlanders are thugs and need to be controlled if you don't want to have less adventurous plants overrun. I have to admit that we probably do spend a disproportionate amount of time gardening this area for this reason. There is one very pretty plant in particular, *Geranium nodosum*, that seeds itself relentlessly

LEFT View entering the Woodland Garden from the Rose Garden with the reservoir visible beyond the gate in the distance
ABOVE View across from the early spring-flowering bed to the large herbaceous bed opposite

throughout this area and we have invented a new verb, 'de-nodosuming': a task which takes a lot of time because the seedlings do not respond to pulling – they have to be dug up. Some people might not mind promiscuous plants in a shady area, but I just mention this as a caution and will deal with others in the section on 'Plants: Friends and Foes'.

I particularly love this part of the garden. It is always a joy to work here, and it is somewhere I find myself more conscious of birdsong and an aura of tranquillity that envelops me. The changing effect of the light during the sun's daily cycle and its position in the sky at different seasons gives extra interest to woodland planting. One of the things that captivates me is the magical effect of shadows in a garden. It is particularly pronounced in this area and definitely adds an extra dimension to the ambience.

ABOVE Bluebells in their blue and white forms
RIGHT (CLOCKWISE FROM TOP LEFT) *Helleborus* × *hybridus* and *Galanthus nivalis*; *Eranthus hyemalis*; *Narcissus* 'Jenny', *Trillium cuneatum*, *Erythronium tuolumnense* and *Primula elatior*; *Geranium* 'Anne Thomson'; *Anemone nemorosa* 'Robinsoniana'

The Water and Bog Gardens

I N ONE SENSE it is perhaps misleading to group these two areas together as the Water Garden was designed and planted in the 1920s and we only created the Bog Garden in the early 2000s. However, because they both contain plants that enjoy damp conditions and one leads to the other, it seems logical to include them in the same chapter. Both areas share the same problem: while parts of the soil are damp, substantial areas are not and yet we have to attempt to give the impression of plants that enjoy the same conditions.

The Water Garden is situated below the Woodland Garden at the end of the pond where the ground falls quite sharply towards the Bog Garden. An outlet from the spring-fed pond feeds the stream running through the Water Garden and continues into the Bog Garden. This area is characterized by paths and streams, quirky stone bridges and small waterfalls, and is paradise for young children. An Atlantic cedar (*Cedrus atlantica*) and white willows (*Salix alba*) which create the shelter belt at this edge of the garden provide partial shade together with large shrubs, including philadelphus, ribes, laurel (*Prunus laurocerasus*), azalea and rhododendron. However, the water is largely confined to the streams, which are edged by stone walls and paths, and it is really only towards the lower part of the Water Garden that the soil is damp, probably as a result of an underground spring. At least in the Bog Garden the water is freer to seep into the surrounding soil, but not sufficiently to ensure the whole area is damp.

View of the house from the Water Garden

The three beds at the top of the Water Garden, above the outlet from the pond, have perfectly normal garden soil. The first of these nearest the pond is our main hellebore bed. These are the most tolerant plants but they do enjoy a reasonable amount of moisture, and during the summer months in dry spells we sometimes have to put the sprinkler here. We had a problem with the hellebores in this bed becoming diseased and generally not flourishing. So in 2017 we sent a soil sample to the Royal Horticultural Society, which came back showing that the proportion of zinc in the soil was far too high. They recommended removing all the plants, taking away the top layer of soil and digging in sterilized compost sold by the local council, which we did. We retained the healthy plants and bought in some new ones, which were then planted during that winter. Their performance has certainly improved, but is still not perfect or as good as some of the smaller groups of hellebores around the garden.

The other two beds contain a number of plants which one might expect to find in a damp area such as *Primula japonica*, *Euphorbia griffithii* 'Fireglow', meconopsis, *Iris sibirica*, hosta and tricyrtis, together with some big-leaved plants – *Hedychium densiflorum* 'Assam Orange', *Hemerocallis fulva* 'Flore Pleno' and *Lilium henryi* – which, given their bulk, suggest plants

that flourish in damp soil. The middle of the three beds has a roughly orange and blue theme. This arose from using orange tulips which would show up from the lawn on the other side of the pond, and this colour continues through the season with *Geum* 'Totally Tangerine', *G.* 'Hannay's' and *G.* 'Coral Supreme', *Primula bulleyana* and *Crocosmia* 'Zambesi', along with the euphorbia, hedychium, hemerocallis and lilium mentioned above. The blue components range from *Pulmonaria angustifolia* 'Munstead Blue', *Omphalodes cappadocica* 'Cherry Ingram', *Polemonium cashmerianum* and *P.* 'Sonia's Bluebell', meconopsis, *Baptisia australis* 'Purple Smoke', *Agastache* 'Blue Fortune', an unnamed campanula and *Hydrangea aspera* Villosa Group.

There is a ledge above the stream where we have plantings of *Dierama pulcherrimum* and *D. pulcherrimum* 'Blackbird' with *Disporum cantoniense* 'Green Giant' and *Disporopsis*

LEFT *Polemonium* 'Sonia's Bluebell', *Papaver cambrica* (Welsh poppy), *Euphorbia griffithii* 'Fireglow' and *Choisya* 'Sundance'
ABOVE *Rhododendron luteum*, *Matteucia struthiopteris* and *Rodgersia aesculifolia* with alchemillas and primulas

pernyi, which together with ferns look pretty overhanging the water. The stream is edged with *Primula japonica* 'Miller's Crimson' interspersed with *Tolmiea menziesii*. On the next level down there are three small beds containing epimediums, ferns, primulas, dicentras, astrantias, hostas, meconopsis and roscoeas. Water feeds into a pool between two of the beds, the sides of which are planted with *Zantedeschia aethiopica* 'Crowborough', *Tricyrtis stolonifera* and *Primula florindae*.

At this point the stream divides around the large bed below, at the top of which is a very old azalea, *Rhododendron luteum*. It has the most wonderful evocative scent which permeates the whole area in May when it is in flower. This is where the soil becomes damper, and there are plantings of *Caltha palustris*, *Lysichiton americanus*, *Euphorbia palustris*, *Primula japonica*, *Matteuccia struthiopteris*, *Iris sibirica* 'Ruffled Velvet', *I. ensata* 'Variegata', *I. pseudacorus*, *I. laevigata* and *I. × robusta* 'Gerald Darby', *Rodgersia aesculifolia* and *R. pinnata* 'Superba', *Zantedeschia* 'Green Goddess' and cultivars of primula, astilbe, lobelia and hosta.

This part of the garden is at its most exciting in May when the purple and deep pink of the Judas tree, *Cercis siliquastrum*, rhododendrons, alliums and primulas are highlighted by the yellow of laburnum, euphorbia, mimulus and azalea and the fresh green of ferns. My particular favourites at this time are the candelabra primulas, but the whole area provides a feast for the senses with the heady scent of the azalea, the vibrant colours, the sounds of water and birdsong, and the almost irresistible temptation to stroke the young foliage of *Acer palmatum* 'Dissectum' beside the path.

In autumn 2020 we decided to take the risk of lifting the precious species *Paeonia mlokosewitschii* (aka Molly the Witch) to a different position. This plant, which has enchantingly beautiful pale yellow flowers with red stems and stamens, is stunning for about three weeks in late May and early June, but later in summer its leaves tend to droop and drop, leaving skeletal remains. As it was occupying a central position in the front of one of my favourite and most visible borders, I thought it would be worth trying to lift and replant it on the north-facing Snowdrop Bank in the Water Garden, where its late summer behaviour would be less obvious. What we hadn't anticipated was the size and depth of the rootball. It took two of us female gardeners' and Richard Green's combined strength to dig it up. It was too big for a wheelbarrow, so we had to heave it on to a heavy-duty trolley to convey it to the Water Garden, and Richard then dug an enormous hole into which we eventually managed to transplant it. So the excitement the following spring while we waited to see if the fat red buds would emerge was considerable. And to our surprise and delight they did.

In gardening one thing often leads to another. And this is an example of how one simple move prompted a renewed look at one of the less interesting parts of the garden and the

pleasure derived from the inspiration to reassess and hopefully improve that area. Hitherto the Snowdrop Bank, which is quite extensive, although delightful in February clothed in snowdrops and into March with primroses, was not particularly interesting for the rest of the spring and summer with a few perennials and a few shrubs. So, after planting *Paeonia mlokosewitschii*, we had a rethink. The existing shrubs included *Weigela* 'Bristol Ruby' and *W.* 'Mont-Blanc', *Kolkwitzia amabilis* and *Viburnum × hillieri*, all flowering early to midsummer, with *Fuchsia magellanica* 'Alba' and *F. magellanica* 'Hawkshead' later on. Since we had managed to acquire some of the new intersectional peonies known as Itoh hybrids, we decided to plant a group to give more early interest after the snowdrops and primroses. So we have now added six of these well spaced out. We then introduced another form of *F. magellanica* called 'Lady Bacon', together with four hydrangeas – *H. paniculata* 'Wim's Red', *H. paniculata* 'Unique', *H. serrata* 'Uzu-Azisai' and *H. macrophylla* 'Merveille Sanguine' – to increase interest for later in the

Lower part of the Water Garden

season. We are now looking forward with a sense of anticipation for these new plants to mature, creating a longer seasonal performance in this area of the Water Garden.

The Bog Garden is approached opposite the summer house at the bottom of the Water Garden. This had been a neglected area of bamboo and elder where the stream had been piped underground to feed ponds in the lower part of the garden. So around 2005 we decided to dig up the pipe and release the water, which now falls gradually in a pebbled stream towards flatter ground, where it collects in a small pool before being piped to the lower pools. After removing the undergrowth, a digger was used to change the contour of the land, allowing a curving path to be created through this area with a wooden bridge crossing the stream. Standing below the bridge provides a delightful view uphill to the Water Garden, while below, the path leads to a view of the Old Orchards.

In the early part of the season there are bergenias, hellebores, erythroniums, leucojum, brunneras, polygonatum, Japanese primulas, hardy geraniums, Siberian irises and hostas. However, in order to differentiate it here from the Water Garden, we selected taller and bigger leafed plants, so by the end of June when they are fully grown, you feel more enclosed by the height of the planting. To achieve this effect we have used *Matteucia struthiopteris*,

Osmunda regalis, *Filipendula camtschatica* and *F. rubra* 'Venusta', *Persicaria polymorpha* and *P. amplexicaulis* 'Rosea', *Darmera peltata*, *Zantedeschia aethiopica* 'Crowborough' and *Z. aethiopica* 'Marshmallow', *Lythrum salicaria* 'Firecandle', *Rodgersia sambucifolia* and *R. aesculifolia*, *Eupatorium purpureum* 'Atropurpureum', *Astilbe chinensis* var. *taquettii* 'Purpurlanze' and *Tricyrtis stolonifera*, plus shrubs in the form of sarcococca, ribes, viburnum, cornus, lonicera, sambucus and phyllostachys.

This is one of the more natural areas of the garden bordering the large meadow often occupied by our Longhorn cattle, with the meandering path then leading above the lower orchard, home to sundry bantams and laying hens, and on to the area below the Old Orchards to a curved bench where visitors can sit and enjoy the view and sound of water falling down the stepped rill.

LEFT View of the Water Garden from the Bog Garden with *Rodgersia aesculifolia* in the foreground
ABOVE Aquilegias, ferns and primulas in the Bog Garden with the foliage of *Persicaria campanulatum* 'Album' in the foreground

The Gravel Garden

I N THE EARLY 1970s my father-in-law acquired two sea lions which he named Bonnie and Clyde. He created a concrete pool for them in part of the Kitchen Garden with a grassed area where they were fed, the whole area being fenced off. On open days there would be two feeding sessions in the afternoons which became an entertainment for visitors. They remained at Coton for four years, during which time my poor mother-in-law had to spend a lot of time defrosting and cutting up herrings for them to eat. But sadly they eventually both died from a virus, whereupon what had been known as the Sea Lion Pool became a home for penguins, and a bridge was built across the water for them. However, this proved to be a less successful exercise than the sea lions had been; eventually the penguins went and the area was turned into what they called a bog garden. This is what we inherited in 1991, and we weren't quite sure what to do with it because there was no bog, just water, and it wasn't a very pretty structure. It would have been an expensive exercise to take it apart, so we decided to retain it. We removed the grass area and fence and covered all the plantable ground with a thick layer of gravel. I am not sure that we actually made it thick enough – I have heard people talk about 13 cm/5 inches of gravel, which is far more than we used – but it seems to work reasonably well. One thing I believe should be avoided if the gravel is to be used for growing plants is putting down a layer of membrane underneath, which is sometimes done in order to suppress the weeds. So that is the genesis of what has become our Gravel Garden. It has two particular advantages.

The Gravel Garden in early June

119

It is an opportunity to have plants that need and look good in their own space, and it is a good medium for encouraging seedlings.

This area is not remotely on the scale of Beth Chatto's wonderful gravel garden, but it enjoys a sunny position and allows us to create a slightly different type of planting space. It occurred to me that in order to distinguish it from the Mediterranean Bank and Herb Garden and given the combination of gravel and water, it would be fun to attempt more of a seaside garden. In some part this was inspired by *Rosa pimpinellifolia* 'Dunwich Rose', a plant from the Suffolk coast and a gift from Richard, our gardener, after a visit there. This then prompted me to plant *Crambe maritima*, known as sea kale, which grows in shingle on the east and south coast. We selected plants which are shown to advantage in their own space rather than competing in a crowded border, some of which might be found growing in seaside conditions.

Euphorbias flourish here and provide excellent structure without getting too large. These include self-sown *E. characias* hybrids, *E.* 'Portuguese Velvet' and *E. stygiana*. It is also a perfect environment for agapanthus, including *A.* 'Navy Blue', *A.* 'Sandringham', *A. campanulatus* 'Albus' and *A.* 'Doctor Brouwer'; likewise eryngiums such as *E.* × *zabelii* 'Violetta' and *E. giganteum*, which seeds itself around. There are *Limonium latifolium*, the sea lavender, and erigerons: *E. karvinskianus* 'Lavender Lady', *E. glaucus* 'Sea Breeze' and *E.* 'Quakeress'. Then there are plants which have been selected because they look good growing in gravel, such as pulsatilla, the horn poppy (*Glaucium flavum*), eucomis, iris, dierama, allium, nerine and dark-leaf forms of hardy geranium. We used to have several miscanthus grasses in the Gravel Garden, but as we found in the Meadow Border, they got too large and needed constant digging up and reducing, so we eventually decided to dispense with them.

In addition to euphorbias, shrubs include prostrate rosemary, potentilla, lavender, perovskia and abelia, and it has also proved to be an ideal spot for species peonies such as *P. tenuifolia*, *P. veitchii* and *P. emodi* early in the season. On the rather thin layer of soil and gravel over the bridge we have planted *Phlox divaricata* subsp. *laphamii* 'Chattahoochee' and *Thymus citriodorus* 'Andersons Gold'.

Growing in the water is *Butomus umbellatus*, the flowering rush. The Gravel Garden backs on to the Rose Walk, so there is a backdrop of pale yellow roses and purple viticella clematis during the main part of summer. Apart from collecting seedlings for the nursery and a certain amount of weeding, it is otherwise less labour intensive than most other parts of the garden.

RIGHT (CLOCKWISE FROM TOP LEFT) *Paeonia veitchii*; *Pulsatilla vulgaris*; *Agapanthus* 'Navy Blue' in the foreground; *Rosa pimpinellifolia* 'Dunwich Rose'; *Paeonia tenuifolia*

The Alpine Terrace and Sinks

I HAVE TO CONFESS that much as I admire alpines in other people's gardens, I am less enthusiastic about them here. Perhaps they seem to be somewhat out of scale with the rest of the garden. Or, perhaps like house plants, they don't give me quite the same thrill as other types of garden plants. However, we do have a terrace wall (built in the 1920s by my husband's grandparents when they were landscaping the garden) that is a perfect site for alpine-type plants. It is in full sun and there is only a thin layer of soil above the stonework of the wall. In one way it works perfectly because so many of the small plants here flower early in the season and create a good show of colour from April into the beginning of June, by which time the Holly Hedge Border separated from it by a narrow strip of lawn starts to perform. I have no idea whether this was the intention nearly one hundred years ago, but if so it was a clever idea and fortuitous for the generations since.

Towards the end of February and into March there are several groups of the enchanting *Iris* 'Katherine Hodgkin', a diminutive pale blue iris with falls streaked with yellow and dark blue. This is followed by blue *Chionodoxa forbesii* and the larger *C.* 'Pink Giant'. By April the delicate white flowers of *Ipheion* 'Alberto Castillo' are joined by *Iris domestica* 'Pumila Campbellii', *Arabis alpina* 'Rosea', *Phlox subulata*, the white daisy flowers of *Rhodanthemum hosmariense*, the heavenly blue, maroon-centred flowers of *Phlox divaricata* subsp. *laphamii* 'Chattahoochee', *Pulsatilla vulgaris*, and the

The Alpine Terrace together with the Holly Hedge Border in August

ABOVE (CLOCKWISE FROM TOP LEFT) *Nepeta racemosa* and *Geranium cinereum* 'Purpureum'; *Phlox divaricata* subsp. *laphamii* 'Chattahoochee' and *Antirrhinum* 'Black Prince'; *Thymus citriodorus* and *Osteospermum* 'Weetwood'; *Iris domestica* 'Pumila Campbellii' LEFT *Phlox divaricata* subsp. *laphamii* 'Chattahoochee', *Dianthus* 'Coconut Sundae', *Erodium chrysanthemum* and *Thymus serpyllum* 'Bressingham Pink'

blue flowers of *Lithodora zahnii* 'Azure-ness', *Nepeta racemosa* and *Convolvulus sabatius*. Interspersed among these are random groups of the annual *Omphalodes linifolia* with tiny white flowers mimicking broderie anglaise.

As the season progresses, there are helianthemum and hardy osteospermum and several of the filigree silver *Artemisia alba* 'Canescens', which is a perfect foil for colours on the wall. In the second half of summer it once again becomes more colourful with a different cast of plants, amongst which are several cultivars of sedum and repeated plantings of the deep pink *Erodium manescavi* and *Fuchsia magellanica* 'Lady Bacon' with its delicate white and pink flowers.

In 2014 we had to do major repairs to the wall, literally taking it down stone by stone and restoring it, and then replanting everything which we had lifted and potted up over winter. This allowed us to remove one or two persistent weeds which had penetrated cracks and been hard to extract and to replant in a more coherent way. It was a major exercise and we were so fortunate to have Yiannis, our one day a week Greek gardener, to do this work so beautifully for us. He has since applied the same skills to rebuilding the walls in the Water Garden and at the foot of the Mediterranean Bank.

We have half a dozen alpine sinks around the garden. These sinks have been covered in wire to hold an outer layer of concrete, giving the effect of stone, and one sink is actually made of stone. Most are on the terraces surrounding the house. One to the left of the old front door is very shallow, and it is a miracle that anything is able to grow in it. But it houses a mix of *Phlox divaricata* subsp. *laphamii* 'Chattahoochee', which survives the winter, along with *Artemisia schmidtiana* 'Nana', *Thymus* 'Silver Posie' and *Sedum spurium*. There is another slightly deeper one on the other side of the door where we grow *Erodium chrysanthum*, *Heuchera* 'Obsidian', *Dianthus* 'Pink Jewel', *Sedum spurium* 'Schorbuser Blut', *Convolvulus cneorum*, *Sempervivum* 'Walcott's Variety' and *Leucojum autumnale*. Around the corner on the south-east terrace are two more sinks, which between them contain *Erodium guttatum*, *Dianthus* 'Elizabethan' and *D.* 'Coconut Sundae', *Thymus* 'Bressingham Pink', *Sisyrinchium* 'E. K. Balls', *Campanula rotundifolia*, *Potentilla* 'White Queen', *Phlox divaricata* subsp. *laphamii* 'Chattahoochee' and *Ranunculus ficaria* 'Randall's White'.

Under the *Rosa* 'Rêve d'Or' just before entering the garden there is a sink, unlike the others, pretty much in the shade. It is deeper and allows us to grow *Helleborus × nigercors* 'Magic Leaves', the delicate maidenhair fern *Adiantum venustum*, *Iberis sempervirens*, *Dryopteris dilatata* 'Lepidota Cristata', *Crassula sarcocaulis*, *Rhodanthemum hosmariense* and *Fuchsia magellanica* 'Hawkshead'.

The Herb Garden

THREE YEARS after we starting gardening at Coton, we decided to remove the rather unattractive corrugated chicken shed in the Kitchen Garden. During the 1950s and early 1960s my parents-in-law had housed chickens here, selling both eggs and chickens to places in London. But later the chickens went and this shed became used for exotic and tropical birds which my father-in-law had started collecting. He added a fruit cage to one side and it became an aviary. On the other side at the foot of the grass slope below the shed he made a canal, fed from a spring, so that the flamingos and other birds which needed cover for the winter could get outside to drink and paddle in the water. We have since discovered that flamingos can cope with extreme cold, and for many years now they have lived outside right through the winter months with free range of the garden. Even if offered shelter they will go into it to eat their food but refuse to stay under cover.

Since this shed was within the confines of the Kitchen Garden, it seemed appropriate to use the space for a Herb Garden. We asked Richard Green, our Head Gardener, to suggest a design. In his inimitable way he amused us by providing six different proposals, each signed 'Capability Green'. We chose the one in place now and it has been a huge success, delighting many visitors over the last three decades. It is good to have an area within the garden that is completely managed by someone other than myself. While the structure of his design is quite formal, the planting is more relaxed, which is entirely appropriate for herbs.

On the top side of the Herb Garden is the Rose Walk, and on the other side we retained the boundary of the Kitchen

View of the Herb Garden in June, showing the house in the background

Garden by planting a yew hedge, which continues the line of the yew hedges at the top of the Rose and Mediterranean Banks. The hedge continues round the end of the Herb Garden to screen the potting shed. (Incidentally, it is a myth that yew hedges take years to establish, hence the tendency to plant leylandii. This one reached full height to match the adjacent hedge within five or six years.) The entrance is flanked by espaliered apple trees. There is a seat at the far end, and on either side he has established standard honeysuckles, using the scented *Lonicera periclymenum* 'Graham Thomas'.

Richard's design is very clever. It consists of eleven beds in all. The ones either side of the seat are a conventional shape and have an edging of origanum (or marjoram to give its common name). The four corner beds are triangular but with an outward curve on the inner-facing edges. The two side beds have an inward-facing curve and all these six beds are edged in *Buxus suffruticosa*, the low-growing box. The two inner beds are arrow-shaped with an inner curve and are edged with hyssop. At the centre of the garden is a small round brick-edged bed of chamomile with a sundial in the middle of it. The idea is that in order to read the sundial people need to stand on the chamomile, which then releases its distinctive fragrance.

However, not everybody gets the point, and you sometimes see people standing on the brick edge with one foot, trying to balance while leaning over to read the sundial!

To fill the beds Richard has used herbs that have traditionally been used for culinary, medicinal and dyeing purposes, although only two fit into the last category: *Isatis tinctoria* or woad, which was historically used as a blue dye, and *Genista tinctoria* or dyer's greenweed as a yellow dye. There are too many plants to enumerate here, but pages 236–7 at the end of this book list the herbs he has planted and what they have been used for and, to some extent, still are. The effect of the planting is delightful, and I know many people find this part of the garden fascinating. They particularly enjoy the espaliered apple blossom in the spring and the later crop of apples. And everyone is intrigued by the spectacle of the standard honeysuckles and keen to know how he established them.

LEFT Entrance to the Herb Garden flanked by espaliered apple trees
ABOVE The Herb Garden in June showing beds edged with *Buxus suffruticosa* in the foreground and with *Hyssopus officinalis* in the centre

Bulbs

OST PEOPLE probably associate bulbs with spring. And while they proliferate in greater numbers at that time, there are bulbs contributing interest to the garden through the summer as well, which to some extent are less well known and used. However, bulbs – or at least plants which tend to be grouped with bulbs – herald the passing of winter and the advent of spring. In our garden the winter aconite, *Eranthis hyemalis*, is first to flower, usually in January. It has a small tuberous root and, if it likes its habitat, provides a carpet of bright yellow flowers into February. It is a wonderful sight, but it does need restricting as it spreads exponentially, which isn't a problem when in flower, but can lead to its foliage camouflaging other low-growing plants as the leaves get larger after flowering and don't disappear until May, by which time they have faded to a rather unattractive yellow. It is best to reduce groups, if desired, when they start to flower or immediately afterwards as their tubers are impossible to see during their dormant season. Snowdrops (galanthus) overlap with winter aconites and, depending on the cultivar and the season, can flower into March. I dearly love snowdrops but would not describe myself as a galanthophile. With one or two exceptions I prefer to see them en masse rather than obsess about the seemingly fine details that distinguish different forms. At Coton they are planted in the Woodland Garden, Water Garden and orchards and throughout the margins of the garden. There is one snowdrop which we inherited without a name. I have been advised by a group of experts that it is unique to this garden and that we are able to call it *G. plicatus* ex Coton Manor. It has broad leaves with a silvered central streak and quite tall large white flowers, altogether like a larger and more impressive version of the normal *G. plicatus*.

In turn, crocus overlap with the flowering of snowdrops. There are unnamed purple ones in the Woodland Garden and a mass of *C. tommasinianus* in shades of purple which have naturalized in the Old Orchards amongst the snowdrops. In sunny spots in March and into April the enchanting pale blue *Iris* 'Katherine Hodgkin' and purple *I. reticulata* will flower, along with blue, pink and white forms of chionodoxa and dwarf forms of narcissus, such as 'Tete-a-Tete' and 'Jumblie'. They precede the main performance of narcissus, which continue into May, finishing with the pheasant's eye, *N. poeticus*. I have a preference for the paler forms of narcissus, in particular

RIGHT (CLOCKWISE FROM TOP LEFT) *Eranthis hyemalis*; *Galanthus elwesii* var. *monostictus*; *Iris* 'Katherine Hodgkin'; unidentified narcissus; *Narcissus* 'Thalia'; *Crocus tommasinianus*

'Jenny' and 'Thalia'. We also have two beautiful delicate single forms, one in white and another in a very pale yellow which frustratingly I have never been able to identify.

Flowering under the copper beech in the woodland there are a number of erythroniums, of which *E. dens-canis*, known as the dog's tooth violet because of its colour and the resemblance of its bulb to a canine tooth, is the first to flower in early March. This is followed by the prolific *E. tuolumnense*, which provides a carpet of yellow amongst the still dormant rodgersias and persicarias in the Bog Garden at this time. Back in the woodland slightly later come the exquisite pale yellow *E.* 'Pagoda' and the creamy white *E. californicum* 'White Beauty' with its mottled foliage. These are swiftly followed by forms of *Anemone nemorosa*, most notably the pale blue 'Robinsoniana' and later the semi-double white 'Vestal', which will still be flowering

ABOVE (CLOCKWISE FROM LEFT) *Erythronium* 'Pagoda'; *Erythronium californicum* 'White Beauty'; *Erythronium dens-canis*
RIGHT *Trillium cuneatum* (left); *Ornithogalum nutans* (right)

into May. At the same time *Trillium cuneatum* produces its long-flowering dark red bracts. Also flowering in the woodland at this time is *Ornithogalum nutans*. This is a beautiful, rather ethereal bulb which produces almost silver-grey hyacinth-like flowers and doesn't have the same tendency to spread everywhere like its fellows *O. umbellatum*, known as the star of Bethlehem, or the taller *O. magnum*, which has attractive flowers but tends to seed madly.

April is the time for tulips, although some will flower into May. I don't know whether it is due to climate change, but the later viridiflora tulips sometimes used to flower until the end of May, and we now find that tulips generally start earlier in April and seldom last beyond the middle of May. Tulips are such a delight. Like so many of my favourite plants they only flower for a short time, but the complexity and variety of their colours and shapes are really breathtakingly beautiful and so often these ephemeral performers, like irises and peonies, provide the greatest pleasure.

There is such a rich selection of tulips to choose from these days that it is easy to find ones that fit into an existing colour scheme in the garden. It is worth looking in catalogues to see

when a tulip flowers as it is possible to have them going for six or seven weeks if they are carefully selected. I plant them in large and repeated groups in borders, usually just one variety, but in two places I use two similar colours which overlap to prolong the flowering period. In the Holly Hedge Border we plant the beautiful 'Finola'. This double pink tulip with splashes of white looks for all the world like a peony, which is entirely appropriate in this herbaceous border. In the central quartered circle of the Rose Garden where there are quite a few plantings of dark-leaf heucheras, I have planted a group of the very dark red double 'Black Hero' in each bed together with two groups of 'Elegant Lady', a pale yellow with a hint of dark red on its outer petals. This both complements and lightens the effect of the recessive dark red. In the Water Garden I have used *Tulipa viridiflora* 'Nightrider', a beautiful purple-pink streaked with green, which works perfectly with *Primula japonica* 'Miller's Crimson' flowering at the same

ABOVE The Holly Hedge Border planted with groups of *Tulipa* 'Finola' in May
RIGHT Lead pots containing *Tulipa* 'Purissima' in the Italian Garden in April

time in that part of the garden. Running through both the Red and Yellow/Blue Borders are plantings of 'Maja' echoing the pale yellow and coinciding with the flowering of *Iris* 'Elegans', *Lupinus* 'Chandelier', *Thermopsis lanceolata* and the shrub *Potentilla fruticosa* 'Vilmoriniana'.

It is also fun when planting tulips in pots to group three or four pots together with colours that enhance each other. I particularly enjoy putting shades of orange and dark red together. So in our entrance yard we might have orange 'Hermitage' and 'Request' with dark red 'Havran' and 'Jan Reus'. Then we might put pots of apricot 'Jimmy' either side of the front door and two more of the same outside the entrance to the restaurant. The two chimney pots outside the cafe are perfect for the shorter 'Prinses Irene'. I never feel that the parrot-type tulips, which are wonderful in a vase, look quite right in a border situation, and they are shown to greater advantage outside in containers. We use two old metal baths and a pair of square wooden tubs for these tulips in the Kitchen Garden area. We also place pots of tulips in many places round the garden, choosing colours that are in harmony with surrounding planting.

One of the most frequently asked questions is, 'Do you dig up your tulips after flowering?' The answer is, 'Yes, we do.' We feel it is important to show them at their best, and the only way

to be sure is to plant new bulbs each year. Some tulips will flower again, but because they divide underground and usually take two to three years, they are in the meantime vulnerable to insect damage and rotting. When we dig them up we put them out for visitors to buy by donating to a local charity, the Northampton Hope Centre, which amongst other things teaches people how to repair garden tools. In turn, we sell their tools in our small shop and they are very popular. I do replant one tulip after digging it up: the viridiflora 'Spring Green'. Its white flowers streaked with green look perfect in the Old Orchards. We plant them singly, and it is interesting to see that in some places where one was planted four may eventually come up. We also have three lots of species tulips which we leave in the ground. On the Mediterranean Bank *T. saxatilis*, which is a delightful shade of pink with splashes of yellow, flowers before the rest. In the Water Garden *T. batalinii* 'Bronze Charm' is a charming low-growing tulip in a soft apricot-yellow. This was planted by one of my gardeners, Sue Mappledorham, as a surprise birthday present. She chose the perfect spot above the stream, and it is often admired by observant visitors. The third is

ABOVE *Tulipa* 'Exotic Emperor' (left); *T.* 'Orange Emperor' (right)
RIGHT *Tulipa sprengeri*

T. sprengeri, which has the purest red flowers and has naturalised along both sides of the Rose Walk. It flowers towards the end of May and is a glorious sight to behold.

We tend to plant tulips in the same position year on year because they are usually in a space that will be occupied by a dahlia or a tender salvia, both of which will need to be lifted in the autumn when the tulips are planted out. However, in some places repeated planting has caused tulip fire, a fungal disease which results in yellowing leaves and poor flowers. To counteract this problem where it has occurred, we plant them in deep black plastic pots and sink them in the ground in groups to prevent the bulbs contacting the soil. It does protect them from becoming diseased, but the performance is never quite as impressive, and in dry conditions we have to remember to water them or they can prove disappointing. Where we can, we try to change the planting position to give the soil a chance to recover. Tulips are a lot of work, but they are so much part of the garden calendar and I would hate to be without them. On balance, their stunning performance makes all the effort worthwhile.

In April in the Woodland Garden, the Old Orchards and the Wildflower Meadow we have groups of the snakeshead fritillary, *Fritillaria meleagris*, that have naturalised. In May the last bulbs to flower in the orchards are *Camassia quamash*, *Narcissus poeticus*, *Ornithogalum nutans* and *Tulipa* 'Spring Green'. This usually coincides with cow parsley (*Anthriscus sylvestris*) and

makes a charming display amongst the cowslips (*Primula veris*) underneath the late blossoms. Elsewhere, there are pale blue *Camassia leichtlinii* and white *C. leichtlinii* 'Alba'. At the same time alliums are starting into flower, starting with *A.* 'Purple Sensation', and in sunnier spots *A. cristophii* and *A. nigrum*. The large purple heads of 'Purple Sensation' are a great addition to the garden after the tulips, but their extensive leaves have a habit of turning yellow just as the flowers open up, so we try to position them behind other plants to disguise it, or remove the leaves, which is a tedious process. The other two alliums are not such a problem.

One of my favourite summer-flowering bulbs which few people recognise is *Galtonia candicans*, known as the summer hyacinth. To me it looks more like a giant snowdrop than a hyacinth. It is very beautiful and we plant it in groups along the front of the Holly Hedge Border, where it readily seeds itself. Then it is the turn of lilies, which I love both for their wonderful flowers and for their scent. The first to appear is in the Woodland Garden, *Lilium martagon*, where it has naturalised in a very shady spot, flowering in its deep pink and white forms. It is so understated and beautiful and seeds willingly. The only other lilies we have are the exquisite *L. regale* and a lesser known one, *L. longiflorum* 'White Heaven', which flowers somewhat later,

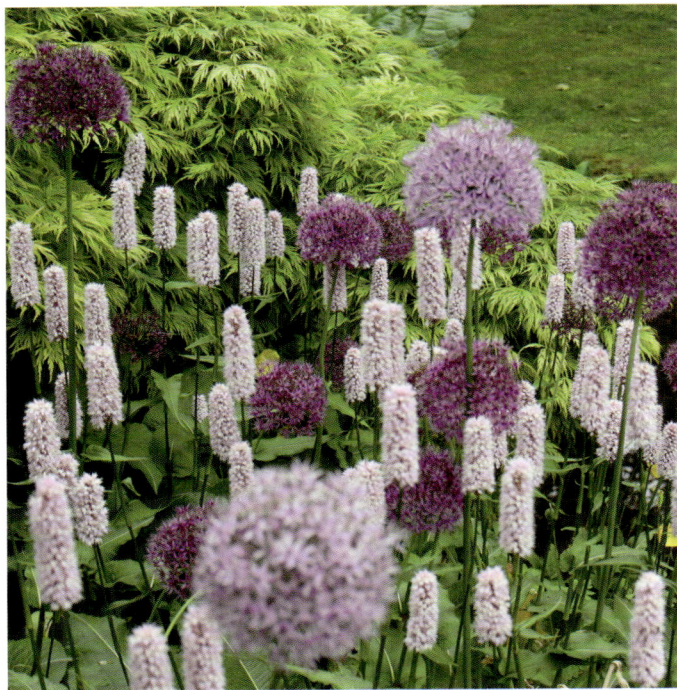

OPPOSITE 'Pheasant's Eye'
Narcissus poeticus with
Fritillaria meleagris in the
Old Orchards
ABOVE LEFT *Camassia leichtlinii*
ABOVE RIGHT *Lilium martagon*
LEFT *Allium* 'Purple Sensation'
amongst *Persicaria bistorta*
'Superbum'

and the orange *L. pardalinum* and *L. henryi*. I used to have more, but the arrival of the lily beetle has reduced my enthusiasm as it is hard work to protect them. In July the late flowering *Allium sphaerocephalon* performs on the Rose Bank in several spaces, and *Crinum × powellii* makes a big statement with its gorgeous pink flower heads at the top of the Rose Bank and the top of the steep bank below the potting shed, where its somewhat untidy foliage is less obvious.

Agapanthus tend to be grouped with bulbs in nursery catalogues and have the common name African lily. They are one of the mainstays of our garden from late July into September, and we use them in several of our sunnier borders. The most popular one that we use and sell is *A*. 'Navy Blue', but there are so many reliable and wonderful blue agapanthus. One of my favourites is *A*. 'Sandringham', which is almost iridescent. We have a very pale mauve form, *A*. 'Windsor Grey', and the white *A. campanulatus* 'Albus', but the one I value most is the pale *A*. 'Blue Moon', which has the particular advantage of not flowering until September, by which time most of the others have gone over. Pale blue is one of the colours I use in the Rose Garden, and with its tall sizeable heads it really shines out amongst the dark red, strong pink and white in late summer. There is some confusion with agapanthus. *A. africanus* with evergreen leaves and the largest flower heads is not entirely hardy and in this country needs to be taken under cover in winter, whereas the herbaceous cultivars which lose their leaves over winter are, by and large, totally hardy and can stay outside in the ground without a problem. I am not sure this distinction is always made clear in nurseries and garden centres, and it is wise to check which type you are buying to ensure it is given the proper treatment.

In late August colchicums start to show their giant crocus-like flowers in shades of mauve, and in September they are followed by *Crocus speciosus* 'Oxonian', which provides a glorious splash of purple in the Woodland Garden. Both these plants, I should add, have the disadvantage of providing unexpected clumps of foliage in spring just when other plants are waking up, so need to be thoughtfully placed.

Another plant which tends to be grouped with bulbs is schizostylis, now renamed hesperantha and commonly known as the kaffir lily. Strictly speaking, this is a rhizome. It comes in shades of red, pink and white and is an invaluable addition to the late summer and autumn garden, flowering from September well into November. Finally, there are nerines, which produce glorious lily-like flowers in a wide range of pinks and white. Nerines like to be baked in the sun, and they will often flower throughout October or sometimes into November.

RIGHT ABOVE *Galtonia candicans* with *Agapanthus* 'Navy Blue'
RIGHT BELOW *Crinum × powellii*

Roses

I AM FREQUENTLY ASKED to name my favourite flower, and I don't suppose I am alone, when pressed, in claiming it to be the rose. I am constantly looking for a space to fit in a new one. It is hard to think of another group of plants which provide such an amazing variety of colour, flower shape, length of flowering time, versatility of habit, scent and, most importantly, pleasure. I have roses growing in borders, as single specimens in the orchards and more naturalised areas of the garden, over low walls, up higher walls, scrambling up and through trees, in pots, and in greatest profusion in areas such as the Rose Walk, Rose Garden and Rose Bank. Fortunately, on the whole, roses thrive in our clay soil.

It has to be said that they also require a considerable amount of work if they are to perform well. In 2006 we removed the roses from the quartered circle in the Rose Garden due to the increasing incidence of rose replant disease. As the four beds had contained 160 roses over a long period of time, it had become the only place where we felt the need to spray, and it was a relief thereafter to abandon the practice altogether. There are a few roses in the garden which suffer attacks from sawfly, usually smaller-flowered varieties such as *Rosa* 'Blush Noisette', 'Cécile Brünner', 'Little White Pet' and 'The Lady Scarman'. However, for the most part we do not suffer too much from other pests or diseases, and I would say that overall the roses have performed better since we ceased using chemicals for feeding or for protection from disease.

Feeding consists of mulching with well-rotted farmyard manure in spring and applying chicken manure pellets to

Rosa banksia 'Lutea' on the south-west terrace

143

repeat-flowering roses just as the first flowering begins to fade. The most time-consuming activity is deadheading and particularly the tedious task of removing yellowing leaves on repeat-flowerers before their second flush. There is also a fair amount of work to do in winter and spring when they need pruning and, in the case of climbers and ramblers, tying in. But I will deal with how we manage that in the section on 'Gardening Techniques'.

The majority in our garden are shrub roses, which I find to be the most versatile and manageable. They can be grown as single specimens or in groups of three or more and, with time and patience, trained as wall shrubs. Their spread and height can vary hugely, so it is worth checking out their potential dimensions before planting, although what the book or nursery says is likely to vary according to the conditions in which they are grown. I love to include shrub roses in border plantings, where they add structure as well as colour and tend to be more resistant to disease than if they are planted in a dedicated rose bed. I do include a number of once-flowering old shrub roses simply because those like 'Cardinal de Richelieu', 'Charles de Mills', 'Fantin Latour', 'Ispahan', 'Madame Hardy', 'Tour de Malakoff', 'Versicolor' and 'William Lobb', plus quite a few more, are all so incredibly beautiful, scented and reasonably long flowering. I can't imagine the garden without them. But it is undoubtedly true that the repeat-flowering roses are better value. It is so hard to select just a few of these, but I would recommend 'Jacqueline du Pré', 'Lady Emma Hamilton', 'Little White Pet', 'Louise Odier', 'Mrs Oakley Fisher', 'Mutabilis', 'De Rescht' and 'Sheelagh Baird' – the last a delightful and perpetual-flowering pink rose with white markings which I inherited with the garden but have never found on any rose grower's list.

In many ways, the most adaptable and reliable group of these shrub roses are the Pemberton hybrid musks. They were bred by a clergyman at the beginning of the twentieth century and include 'Buff Beauty', 'Cornelia', 'Felicia', 'Moonlight', 'Penelope' and 'Prosperity'. They are perfect shrub roses in pink, yellow and white. They repeat well, are scented and have attractive flower shapes. If I am attempting to train a rose against a wall or on the side of a pergola, I would choose one of this group. It will take longer than using a climber to reach any height, but it will flower and branch from the bottom upwards, whereas a climber has a more vertical inclination and can become rather bare and woody at the base while its flowers want to reach for the sky. Where a wall is high and there is plenty of space to spread branches horizontally, then it is fine to use a climber, although it will be necessary to remove older branches from the base now and then to encourage new growth and avoid the woody look.

RIGHT (CLOCKWISE FROM TOP LEFT) *Rosa* 'Francis E. Lester'; *R. gallica* 'Versicolor' (syn. *R. mundi*); *R. damascena* 'Ispahan'; *R.* 'Prosperity'; *R.* 'Tour de Malakoff'; *R.* 'Lady Emma Hamilton'

It is impossible to discuss the subject of roses without mentioning the iconic rambling rose flowering in June on the front of the old part of the house, photographs of which have become particularly identified with this garden. We suspect that it was already planted on the house when it was purchased in the 1920s. My mother-in-law always referred to it as *Rosa* 'Coton Manor'. Various rose experts have suggested different names, and we believe that it is probably *R. multiflora* 'Platyphylla', also known as 'Seven Sisters' or *R. multiflora* 'Grevillei'. There are three specimens on the walls. It opens in a deep magenta-pink gradually fading through lighter shades to lilac-pink. It is highly scented and makes a stunning picture against the honey-coloured stone of the house.

If you are trying to grow a rose up a tree, a rambler is probably best. The ones which do particularly well in our garden are 'Apple Blossom', 'Chevy Chase', 'Francis E. Lester' and 'Rambling Rector', while 'Phyllis Bide' and 'Purple Skyliner' are excellent repeat-flowering ramblers for lower growing situations. On our Rose Walk we originally planted a number of the climbing 'Madame Alfred Carrière' interspersed with 'Desprez à Fleurs Jaunes' and 'Sombreuil'. None of these proved to be ideal. After several years they became woody, and

after its first flowering 'Madame Alfred Carrière' sent up long stems of vegetative shoots waving above the framework which we had to climb up and cut back, with only a poor second flowering. It was clearly not the best place for that rose, which I have seen performing so well in different situations elsewhere. So a while ago we removed all these roses. Growing amongst them we had purple *Clematis* 'Etoile Violette' and *C.* 'Jackmanii Superba', so I chose pale yellow roses to provide a pleasing colour contrast. To grow up and over the structure we chose the repeat-flowering, pale yellow rambler 'Malvern Hills', together with shrub roses 'Buff Beauty' and 'Ghislaine de Féligonde' to clothe the sides of the walk in shades of pale to apricot-yellow. The last I would rate as one of my favourite and most reliably long-flowering roses; as you deadhead the first flush there are already new buds waiting to open, and it seems, for us at least, to be disease free. We are still waiting for 'Malvern Hills' to cover the

LEFT *Rosa multiflora* 'Platyphylla' (Seven Sisters' rose)
ABOVE *Rosa* 'Malvern Hills' and *Clematis viticella* 'Etoile Violette'

top part of the arching rose frame, but I have long since learnt from experience that patience is needed in gardening, and when something does eventually perform as hoped for, it is even more rewarding. I suspect that because the clematis were already established and the roses are planted close to them, this may have caused them to struggle somewhat. Rose growers always advise against planting clematis with a rose before the rose is properly established, but in this instance the clematis were there first.

Climbing roses are less rangy than ramblers and usually provide a second flowering. Perhaps the most beautiful one we have is 'Cooper's Burmese'. With lovely single white flowers in June, it has almost evergreen foliage and looks a picture on another wall of the house. This probably draws more comment from visitors than any other rose in the garden. While it flowers for a long while and they gradually fade to pink, it sadly does not repeat. On the opposite side of the recess in which it is planted is 'Bengal Beauty', with crimson single flowers from May onwards,

ABOVE LEFT *Rosa* 'Dorothy Perkins'
ABOVE RIGHT *Rosa* 'Bengal Beauty'
RIGHT *Rosa* 'Cooper's Burmese'

a shrub which can be grown as a small climber. Another particular favourite is 'Autumn Sunset', which despite its name starts flowering in early June. Although the rose growers describe it as a shrub, we grow it as a climber in one place with considerable reach. It produces generous trusses of flowers in shades of apricot-yellow and repeats with a good second flush. Other climbers in the garden include 'Blush Noisette', 'City of York', 'Climbing Cécile Brünner', 'Climbing Lady Hillingdon', 'Meg', 'Mermaid' and 'Tess of the d'Urbervilles'.

In some instances we provide a structure as support for roses that need it. These are constructed by our Head Gardener, Richard Green. He uses hazel for the upright parts of the framework and woven bands of willow to hold the structure together. This enables us to support shrub roses such as 'Fantin-Latour', 'Reine des Violettes', 'Tour de Malakoff' and 'William Lobb', so that their branches don't collapse on other plants. The advantage of tying in the branches horizontally is that it encourages more buds to break, resulting in more flowers. These natural frameworks provide interest in the winter months. We have also used them where we want to contain climbers and ramblers as shrubs in borders, as we have done with 'Albéric Barbier' and 'Autumn Sunset'.

I love to plant roses in the outer reaches of the garden. Rugosas are ideal for this purpose. There are groups of *R. rugosa* 'Alba' and 'Scabrosa' bordering the meadow and a hedge of 'Roseraie de l'Haÿ' at the bottom of the orchards. *R. californica* 'Plena' is also perfect for these areas, with its wonderful array of very scented, deep pink double flowers on long, arching stems. We grow 'Dorothy Perkins' with its mass of small pink flowers up a tree beside the gate to the Wildflower Meadow. In the orchards we have groups of 'Nevada' and its pink sport, 'Marguerite Hilling', 'Brewood Belle', 'Chevy Chase' and 'Climbing Cécile Brünner' up trees, while 'Constance Spry' and 'Madame Hardy' are grown like a spider with their long stems tied down to a hazel framework to encourage increased flowering. Finally, I should not forget the value of having roses to pick for the house. We have a small number in our vegetable plot which are intended for this purpose, and, of course, there are plenty that I can raid from the garden without it being too noticeable.

LEFT *Rosa* 'William Lobb'
ABOVE *Rosa* 'Roseraie de l'Haÿ'

Clematis and other Climbers

I AM SURE there is a hardly a garden in the country without at least one clematis. They are one of the most beautiful, varied and long-performing plant groups available to gardeners. Some, such as *C. cirrhosa* 'Freckles', can flower from November to February, while others start performing in spring, more continue through summer and the last ones, such as *C. rehderiana*, are still flowering in October. There are clematis for sunshine and shade and many intermediate ones which will do well in either situation. Perhaps the one common factor is that they do not like to dry out, although provided they are planted with their roots reasonably deep, once established they will tolerate most drought situations. They are mostly known as climbers, but they also come in herbaceous and semi-herbaceous forms, the latter usually needing some form of support; then there are those like *C. × jouiniana*, which can be useful either as a climber or as ground cover. They can be grown successfully in pots if the right cultivar is selected, and they are lovely scrambling up trees, with roses, over shrubs which have finished flowering and on low walls. Some are scented, such as *C. × aromatica* and 'Betty Corning', and they come in a huge range of colours.

Apart from the winter-flowering 'Freckles' mentioned above, we have very few early clematis in the garden. I did inherit two scented montanas on the walls of the entrance yard – the white 'Wilsonii' and the pink 'Elizabeth' flowering from late May into June – they were both lovely but tended to overwhelm other plants and I finally got rid of them. We have since planted 'Marjorie' – a subtle cream and salmon semi-double flower – on the other side of the wall, so that when it climbs over it is less inclined to swamp the plants growing underneath. We also have two early clematis on the walls either side of the steps leading from the entrance terrace to the main lawn. They are 'Guernsey Cream' (with large, completely stunning creamy white flowers with a hint of green) and 'Lemon Beauty' (with lime-yellow, nodding, bell-shaped flowers), both of which are out from mid-May into early June.

I think it is sometimes confusing for people to understand the difference between the three traditional groups of climbing clematis. Generally, Group 1 includes alpinas, montanas and macropetalas, plus a few others; Group 2 includes the larger-flowered cultivars (of which we

RIGHT ABOVE *Clematis* 'Jackmanii Superba'
RIGHT BELOW *Clematis* 'Guernsey Cream'

only have one), and Group 3 is mainly the texensis and viticella groups. These descriptions are a simplification as so many more cultivars have been bred in recent years, not all of which fit into the above categories. We have a lot of climbing clematis in the garden, predominantly the third group and mainly viticellas. I prefer these small-flowered clematis because they perform for much longer than the other two groups and are much easier to manage: they simply need to be cut almost to the ground sometime in late winter or early spring. Groups 1 and 2 require general tidying up and occasional hard cutting back, which is a less exact science.

The only Group 2 clematis I grow is 'Nelly Moser', a popular large-flowered cultivar with pink and white striped markings. Interestingly, we inherited this clematis in a sunny position on the side of our garden room, where it regularly got burnt by the sun. So I moved it to a shadier position on a silver birch tree at the top of the Water Garden, where it flowered well until the birch came down in a storm. We rescued the clematis and replanted it on another silver birch in a glade in the Dells, where it looks quietly romantic for those observant enough to notice it.

It seems invidious to name my favourite clematis because they are all so lovely, but some are a particularly special colour, others flower for a very long period, while still others have a special flower shape or wonderful seed heads. One of my top ones is the Polish 'Romantika' – the darkest, almost black, velvety purple. Set against a pale yellow rose, this is one of my very favourite combinations. 'Huldine' is exquisite. It has pearly white flowers, the underside of the petals is mauve, it is extremely vigorous, and it flowers for a long time too. 'Perle d'Azur' is a beautiful, reasonably long-flowering blue; 'Black Prince' is a very long-flowering small dark purple, extremely vigorous, and a perfect foil for pale-coloured companion planting. *C. viticella* 'Odoriba' has pink bells with white centres, flowers for a long time, and looks wonderful with the similar-coloured flowers of *Rosa* 'Tour de Malakoff'. One of the most reliable and beautiful clematis we have is *C. texensis* 'Princess Diana', with strong pink bells and a very long flowering period. I cannot leave out the larger-flowered purple 'Jackmanii Superba', which puts on an amazing show in July and August, or the Polish 'Błękitny Anioł' (Blue Angel) with its lovely pale blue flowers. The list can seemingly go on for ever because we are so spoilt for choice.

In some ways the most valuable clematis for gardeners are the semi-herbaceous ones. They are relatively easy to manage, do not take up much space, and if deadheaded regularly will

RIGHT (CLOCKWISE FROM TOP LEFT) *Clematis* 'Nelly Moser'; *C.* 'Perle d'Azur' and *C.* 'Venosa violacea'; *C. montana* 'Marjorie'; *C. texensis* 'Princess Diana'

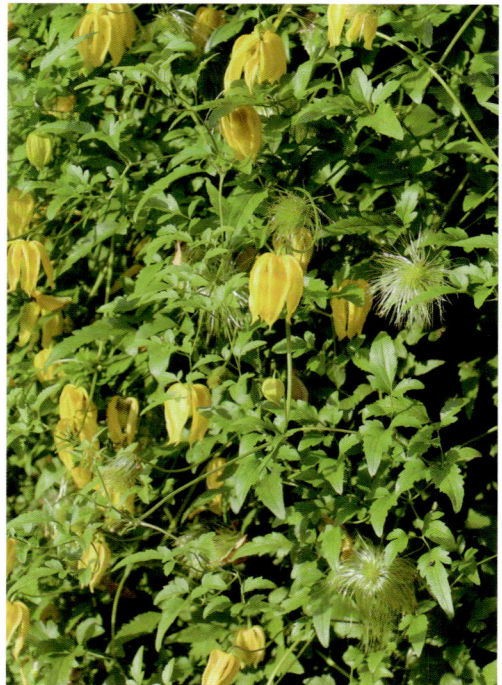

flower for a large part of the summer. The first one we have is *C. recta*, which produces a mass of small white flowers early in the season and definitely needs support if it is not going to sprawl over surrounding plants. We are particularly fond of the lovely blue form of *C. integrifolia* with its beautiful bell-shaped flowers. To be shown to best advantage it also needs some support. Once they attain a mature size, we use the same type of structure as for roses, but they can take quite a while to become established and a wigwam of hazel branches works well for the first few years. We have several plantings of the pink form, *C. integrifolia* 'Rosea', but they do not reach the same height or stature and can cope with a smaller framework. Another good one in this group is the purple 'Petit Faucon', which has a similarly pleasing habit. But, perhaps the most impressive is *C. × durandii* with deep blue, saucer-shaped flowers with contrasting golden anthers, which if deadheaded regularly really will flower throughout the summer. This works well on a tallish wigwam. There is also the popular 'Arabella' with masses of small bluish purple flowers.

Less well known are the truly herbaceous clematis which do not need support and behave like normal border plants. The main type is *C. heracleifolia*. There are various forms of this, and the one we favour is 'Cassandra'. This grows to about 0.9 m/3 ft tall and spreads well. It has intense deep blue flowers starting in July and continuing into September. It has good foliage and the flowers are scented. It would certainly count as one of my top ten border plants.

We have three rather different late flowering clematis, although one of these, *C. tangutica* 'Lambton Park', starts flowering in June. It just continues flowering along with producing beautiful seed heads until after we close at the end of September. It has the species' typical nodding, bright yellow, bell-shaped flowers, and unlike other clematis it isn't necessary to deadhead the seed heads as they don't stop it producing new flowers. It is scented and flourishes in a sunny position. Another late performer is *C. × jouiniana*, which is a vigorous, scrambling plant with pretty pale blue flowers. It does not cling, so needs to be either supported or allowed to spread. As it starts flowering in the later part of summer, it can be used to cover other plants that have gone over, where it will continue for a long time. It needs to be planted in a sunny position. The third late flowering clematis we have is *C. rehderiana*, known for its scent as the primrose clematis. It starts flowering in August and continues well into October with masses of pale yellow flowers and is very vigorous.

TOP *Clematis × jouiniana* climbing over *Rosa* 'Autumn Sunset'
FAR LEFT *Clematis heracleifolia* 'Cassandra'
LEFT *Clematis tangutica* 'Lambton Park'

OTHER CLIMBERS

I often wish that I had more walls for even more roses, clematis and other climbers, but most of our house and garden wall space is already well subscribed so we have only a few alternative climbers. We have two types of the Mediterranean evergreen trachelospermum: the smaller leaved *T. asiaticum* and the larger leaved *T. jasminoide*s. They both produce small, scented white flowers and adorn walls on different parts of the terrace surrounding the house. There are also two grape vines on the house walls, *Vitis vinifera* 'Brandt' and *V. vinifera* 'Purpurea'. Both have handsome foliage which turns a wonderful colour in the autumn.

Probably one of the things people remember about the garden at Coton is the wonderful wisteria display in May. We inherited one very old and established wisteria, which we suspect had been on the wall when the house was bought in the 1920s because it had the most enormous trunk which spread halfway across the terrace. With some misgivings we cut a substantial part of this back shortly after we took on the house and garden as it really got in the way of visitors walking round that part of the terrace. Amazingly, it recovered and continued to flourish, providing a spectacle each year with its massive amount of blue racemes of highly scented flowers. We then planted another one – *W. floribunda* 'Domino' – on the corresponding wall of the house, which grew and flowered surprisingly quickly after only a few years. Together they made a fabulous show. However, in 2021 the old one showed signs of weakening with fewer flowers and much less leaf growth. We left it to see what would happen in 2022, but clearly it was dying so with a huge feeling of sadness we cut it down, and when it came time to remove the trunk it didn't provide any resistance. We assume that it just died of old age.

Wisteria on the south-east side of the house

RIGHT *Trachelospermum asiaticum*
OPPOSITE (CLOCKWISE FROM TOP LEFT) *Wisteria brachybotrys* f. *albiflora* 'Shiro-kapitan'; *Tropaeolum speciosum*; *Trachelospermum jasminoides*; *Vitis coignetiae*

We have now planted another 'Domino' in its place to match the existing one. Meanwhile, in the Bog Garden we have trained a white wisteria up a cherry tree. This is *W. brachybotrys* f. *albiflora* 'Shiro-kapitan'. It flowers quite a lot later than the blue ones, but it is a delightful sight and has reached quite a height.

On the wall of the restaurant in the Stable Yard there is a very vigorous *Akebia quinata*, commonly known as the chocolate vine. This flowers in April into May and has many clusters of very pretty dark red flowers, ostensibly smelling of chocolate, with attractive foliage. Growing up one of the Irish yews surrounding the main pond we have the scarlet-flowering *Tropaeolum speciosum*, which is a spectacular sight when flowering well. In recent times it has been less impressive, maybe because we were robbing some of its fleshy white roots for propagation. However, to my relief, after a few years of leaving it alone, it is showing signs of producing its beautiful flowers again. The only other climbers we can lay claim to in the garden are ivy, which in its varied forms can make an attractive covering on a wall, and the crimson glory vine, *Vitis coignetiae*, which is growing on a fence at the side of the Goose Park and has made its way up an ash tree on the other side of the fence. As its name implies, this vine turns brilliant shades of red in the autumn.

Trees and Shrubs

WE WERE FORTUNATE to inherit many interesting trees planted in the 1920s. As I have mentioned, I think mature trees in the garden contribute to its atmosphere. They offer a sense of permanence; they provide a framework for the garden which gives its spaces a feeling of intimacy, and they create shady areas which are much appreciated on a hot day. Individually, they are beautiful with different shapes and foliage, and in winter it is a joy to be able to appreciate their silhouettes and the tracery of their branches. Needless to say, given that many of the trees were planted a century ago, we have lost some of them, mainly the white willows (*Salix alba*) planted as a shelter belt on the south-east side of the garden, although for the time being with the help of a strong laurel hedge (*Prunus laurocerasus*) underneath them, just enough remain standing to give protection from that direction.

From a design point of view, I think the most significant tree planting which they undertook is the six Irish yews, *Taxus baccata* 'Fastigiata', round the main pond, two below the steps from the terrace and two more in the entrance yard. These architectural trees must have suffered from neglect during the war years and now, nearly one hundred years after they were planted, they have acquired distinctly idiosyncratic shapes that in many ways are quirkily charming and in keeping with the garden, which defies any attempt at geometry or straight lines. However, they are quite a challenge when it comes to annual pruning – I can hardly bear to watch the perilous process involved.

View of the pond in autumn, showing golden *Ginkgo biloba* on the right, evergreen *Cedrus atlantica* at the far end and specimens of *Taxus baccata* 'Fastigiata' (Irish yew) at intervals round the pond

The tree which seems to attract the most attention is in the centre of the Stable Yard. It is a very large black walnut, *Juglans nigra*. It provides a perfect canopy for those sitting at tables underneath, sheltering them from the sun and sometimes the rain. We know this tree was planted when the stables were built. In America there are walnut plantations where they are grown for making furniture. Perhaps it was their American heritage which inspired the grandparents to plant this tree. Whatever the reason, we are immensely grateful to them, and it obviously helped that it started life with plenty of horse muck to hand.

Another tree of American origin which they planted is the tulip tree, *Liriodendron tulipifera*. We believe that this now reaches about 27–30 m/90–100 ft and provides wonderful shade in the Woodland Garden. At the bottom of the main lawn below the house there is a huge horse chestnut, *Aesculus hippocastanum*, and a vast beech, *Fagus sylvatica*, on the bank below. They also bequeathed us a number of Norway maples, *Acer platanoides*. They are beautiful trees, up to 18 m/60 ft tall with typical green, palmate-lobed leaves which turn a glorious shade of yellow early in autumn. The downside to these trees is the red stem suckers which they produce in large areas around the base of the trunk. In spring these are quite attractive and people often ask what they are, but from a management point of view they are a nuisance, and we constantly have to hack them back to prevent them spreading into planted areas.

In the Woodland Garden, apart from the tulip tree and a splendid copper beech, *Fagus sylvatica* f. *purpurea*, there are beech, chestnut, birch and other woodland trees. I particularly love the effect of the shadows cast by these trees. In the lower part of the garden they planted quite a few wild cherries, *Prunus avium*, which in a good summer produce the most delicious small, dark red cherries, useful for making jam.

In many ways their most valuable planting was the introduction of beech trees in the Bluebell Wood; at least we assume that they date back to that period. In the 1990s, when we applied to what was then MAFF (Ministry of Agriculture, Fisheries and Food) for a grant to thin the trees in the wood and plant more, initially we were informed that they couldn't supply beech as it wasn't a native Northamptonshire tree. However, once one of their officials had visited and established that it was ancient woodland, they obliged and we were able to replant. Beeches are the perfect canopy for bluebells. The lime green of their emerging leaves sets off the intensity of the blue flowers below; they allow the right amount of light through; their

RIGHT ABOVE *Juglans nigra* (black walnut) in the Stable Yard
RIGHT BELOW View from south-west terrace showing large specimens of *Aesculus hippocastanum* (horse chestnut) right and *Fagus sylvatica* (beech) left

smooth vertical trunks give an almost cathedral-like effect, adding to the spiritual feeling of the wood; and their foliage provides ideal leaf mould for the bluebells to flourish.

The year 1987 was my parents-in-law's golden wedding anniversary and one of their presents was a *Ginkgo biloba*, an ancient Chinese tree sometimes known as the maidenhair tree. To quote the Royal Botanic Gardens Kew website, 'This is one of oldest living tree species in the world.' It is planted at one end of our main pond and is very attractive with its unusual fan-shaped leaves. It took many years to put on much growth, but has now reached a considerable height.

In the late 1960s when they added part of the field below into the garden, they planted some interesting trees into this area. Amongst them were the paperbark maple, *Acer griseum*, a sweet gum, *Liquidambar styraciflua*, and the Indian bean tree, *Catalpa bignonioides*. I am happy to say that the first two still survive, but sadly the catalpa succumbed to verticillium wilt many years ago. They also planted some interesting fruit trees: namely, a quince, *Cydonia oblonga*, a medlar, *Mespilus germanica*, and a white mulberry, *Morus alba*. The quince provides a plentiful crop of fruit from which we make and sell both quince cheese and jelly. The medlar was uprooted in a storm; I believe they are quite shallowly rooted. We replanted another one in a

more sheltered position and the same thing happened again. So we have abandoned medlars. Apparently, the reason that many gardens belonging to houses dating back to the seventeenth century have a black mulberry tree in them is because King James I was keen to introduce mulberry trees to create a silk industry in this country. He encouraged those with good-sized gardens to plant them. However, he mistakenly imported the black rather than the white mulberry trees that silkworms depend upon, and so the silk industry was never established. Our own white mulberry – which produces delicious small black fruit, rather sweeter than the black mulberry – nearly came to grief some years ago when a split developed in the trunk into which rain penetrated and the tree started to die off. We didn't know whether to cut it down altogether and plant a new one, or to give it a radical chop. So we decided to more or less stool it at about 0.9–1.2 m/3–4 ft and see what happened. This left a fairly lop-sided trunk

LEFT The Bluebell Wood in late summer
ABOVE View of the house from the Goose Park with *Sequoiadendron giganteum* (Wellingtonia) top left and *Cydonia oblonga* (quince) right

arrangement which didn't look at all promising. However, to our surprise and delight, the next summer a few shoots appeared; within about four or five years it had somehow miraculously recovered its original beautiful shape and is now producing fruit again.

During our three decades of tenure in the garden we have introduced quite a few more trees. My favourite is the katsura, *Cercidiphyllum japonicum*, which is the most elegant shape. It is multi-trunked and has heart-shaped green leaves which both turn a very attractive gold colour in early autumn and give off an aroma of caramel or burnt toffee – or so I am told, but sadly I am not able to detect and enjoy it, a sense of smell being so subjective. The lower branches are a favourite perching point for our flock of Mille Fleur Barbu d'Uccle bantams.

We decided to add more specimen trees into the large green space in the lower part of the garden which became known as the Goose Park, although there have been no geese here since the early 1990s. Amongst these are weeping alder, *Alnus* incana 'Pendula'; Himalayan birch, *Betula utilis* subsp. *jacquemontii*; wedding cake tree, *Cornus controversa* 'Variegata'; cut-leaf beech, *Fagus sylvatica* 'Laciniata'; crab apples, *Malus* 'Butterball' and *M. robusta* 'Red Siberian'; Persian ironwood, *Parrotia persica*; snakebark maple, *Prunus serrula*; and great white cherry, *Prunus* 'Tai-Haku'. Also planted here are some generous gifts: a Wellingtonia, *Sequoiadendron giganteum*, given to us by a visitor to the garden, and a Chinese red birch, *Betula utilis* subsp. *albosinensis*, given to us by Roy Lancaster when he came here to deliver a lecture several years ago. We used to buy pots from a pottery near Rugby and the owner kindly gave us a young tulip tree, *Liriodendron tulipifera*, because it had outgrown the pot in his yard. He delivered this in his car around twenty years ago and it is now about 12 m/40 ft high. I often find myself pausing with a smile when passing these trees to remember the kind people who gave them to us.

SHRUBS

There was a time not so long ago when shrubs were rather unfashionable. However, it is hard for me to imagine gardening without taking advantage of the many attractive and versatile shrubs that are available today. It is fair to say that apart from roses I do not have that many shrubs in my herbaceous borders. But there are several areas of the garden where we do use them, such as the Woodland Garden, Water Garden, the Dells, Mediterranean Bank, Rose Bank, Goose Park and on the house walls.

The main reasons why I don't plant many shrubs in herbaceous borders is partly that over time they get too big and can eventually mask and overpower neighbouring plants, and, second, they only flower for a relatively short time and can look fairly dull afterwards. One exception I make is for tree peonies, which on the whole have beautiful foliage. I tend to use the group of shrubs which flower on the current year's growth and need cutting back in spring,

allowing me to control their growth to some extent, largely those which flower in the second part of summer for a generous length of time. These include deciduous forms of ceanothus like *C.* 'Gloire de Versailles' and *C.* 'Henri Desfossé', *Caryopteris × clandonensis* 'Heavenly Blue', *Ceratostigma willmottianum*, *Senecio greyi* (now known as *Brachyglottis* 'Sunshine'), the hardy magellanica form of fuchsia, buddleja, shrubby forms of hypericum and the arborescens and paniculata forms of hydrangea, to name a few.

Perhaps the most useful of all are the many different coloured forms of shrubby salvia, mostly emanating from Central and South America. Apart from benefitting from being cut back in the spring and some deadheading in the summer months, they require very little attention. In an average winter, most prove hardy, and there are only a handful which we lift for winter protection each year (in some cases, merely to provide space for tulip planting). Amongst the sixty or so cultivars we have, I would rate the tall, deep pink *S. involucrata* as one of the most hardy and spectacular plants for a sunny border; likewise, tall, dark purple *S.* 'Amistad' is

Rosa 'Ghislaine de Féligonde' and *Philadelphus* 'Belle Etoile'

hardier than many people think because in spring after being cut back it is the slowest to show signs of leafing up, and I think is often mistakenly dug up on the assumption that it is dead. The other advantage of making use of these types of shrub is that as they gain height after being cut back in the spring, they can be used to mask earlier plantings which have gone over.

One group which I really value is euphorbias, though, strictly speaking, these are classed as subshrubs. They come in many shapes and sizes, some with green or glaucous foliage and others with silver. And there are euphorbias for sun, shade, damp and dry areas so they are incredibly useful in the garden. Their lime green chartreuse-like flowers or bracts are a very effective foil for the purples, pinks and blues in spring and early summer. It is hard to imagine gardening without them. With the larger characias forms we cut the flower stems right down, usually in early June as soon as they show signs of going over, making sure that any bare flesh is covered because their milky sap is notorious for causing skin reactions and especially dangerous if it gets into the eyes. After the flower stems have been removed, the shrub reverts to its bluish green foliage, from which the following year's flowers will emerge, but which in this form is still a very attractive addition to the border.

It is important to select shrubs which have both spring and autumn interest where possible, or which have attractive foliage, such as choisya, myrtle and cotinus. Many flowering shrubs such as skimmia, viburnum, amelanchier, azalea, cotinus, stephanandra and some hydrangeas give a glorious burst of autumn colour and some also produce berries.

There are a number of evergreen flowering shrubs which can cope with relatively dry shade, most of which tend to flower from late winter into spring. In our garden there are several varieties of sarcococca, which have small, highly fragrant white- or pink-tinged flowers through the late winter months. A wonderful waft of scent emerges from just a few stems picked for the house. In the garden it is also one of those smells which you catch in the air without having to put your nose to the flowers. *Daphne bholua* 'Jacqueline Postill' has beautiful scented flowers through January and into March. These flowering shrubs need to work hard to attract pollinating insects in winter – hence their strong fragrance. Later flowering evergreens include cultivars of choisya, which seem to flourish in fairly deep shade, still producing white flowers, which together with their light-reflective foliage can light up a dark area. Skimmia is another evergreen candidate for shade with white or red flowers, followed later by berries. And if your soil is slightly acidic like ours, some rhododendrons can be included in this group too.

RIGHT (CLOCKWISE FROM TOP LEFT) *Hydrangea preziosa*; *Ceratostigma willmottiana*; *Paeonia* (Itoh hybrid) 'Sonoma Blessing'; *Escallonia bifida*

ABOVE *Cornus* 'Eddie's White Wonder' in early June and *Cercidiphyllum japonicum* (katsura tree) on right

RIGHT *Cornus* 'Eddie's White Wonder' in autumn

But probably deciduous shrubs form the majority of flowering bushes in our garden. The first to perform for us in early spring is witch hazel, *Hamamelis × intermedia* 'Diane'. This has rusty orange flowers in late January and early February which meld beautifully with the surrounding carpet of fallen beech leaves. And in late autumn the leaves turn a glorious shade of coppery orange. One of my favourites, the flowering currant *Ribes sanguineum* 'White Icicle', so perfectly named, is planted in several places round the garden and is happy to grow in shady and fairly dry conditions where it shows up beautifully in early spring. Another white-flowering shrub for late spring which is very popular is *Exochorda × macrantha* 'The Bride', and of course there are the tree peonies with their transient, exquisitely fragile scented flowers in delicate shades with characteristic dark central markings – one of the truly ephemeral moments of early summer. We have a number, including *Paeonia delavayi*, *P. delavayi ×* (*× suffruticosa*), *P. × suffruticosa* and *P. rockii* hybrids. However, the one which stands out for me from all the others in late May and early June is *Cornus* 'Eddie's White Wonder'. This shrub has beautiful white bracts with small green centres and flowers for a decent length of time, drawing huge admiration from all who see it. Amongst others there are many different viburnums, deutzias, weigelas and philadelphus to enjoy.

Later in summer there is an interesting range of hydrangeas which – like so many other later performing plants – flower for a very long time and are therefore particularly worth including in any garden scheme. Also at this stage of the season we have the wonderful myrtle, *Myrtus communis*, with fluffy white flowers, *Abelia × grandiflora* and *Escallonia bifida*, the latter two being hugely attractive to butterflies and bees. We inherited a large *Clerodendron trichotomum* in the Rose Garden and lived with it for several years. It is one of those shrubs which has scented flowers but rather unattractive smelling foliage, and its worst feature, like all other clerodendrons, is a tendency to sucker. Finally, when it started surfacing through and above the 1.8 m/6 ft adjacent holly hedge, we decided to get rid of it, though it took several years to eliminate the suckers. However, we have planted *Clerodendron bungei* on one of the islands on the pond, where it is thankfully contained and we can enjoy its deep pink flower heads from a safe distance!

The other invaluable shrub category is those grown for their foliage and often used for topiary or hedging. In this garden it is mainly common box, *Buxus sempervirens*, and its lower growing form, *B. sempervirens* 'Suffruticosa', *Phillyrea angustifolia* and common holly, *Ilex aquifolium*. This is not a topiary garden, but we do have a number of simple shapes carved out of these shrubs which contribute to the structure, particularly in the winter months.

These trees and shrubs are far from a comprehensive list of those in our garden, but just the ones we particularly value and receive the most comments from visitors.

Pots, Containers and Troughs

M Y MOTHER-IN-LAW accumulated an eclectic collection of tender pelargoniums, most of which I am thankful to say we still have three decades later. Over the years we have considerably increased the range of pelargoniums and other tender plants because they provide a glorious splash of colour, particularly valuable in the second part of summer when some herbaceous plants are going over and we are waiting for the second performance of repeat-flowering roses. There was a fashion in the 1980s and 1990s to mix a lot of different plants in large pots, which, if well done, can be very effective, but over the years I have increasingly come to favour pots with plants of just one variety. In some cases I group several pots together with sympathetic or similar colours. This enables us to remove a pot where the flowers have gone over, whereas if they are mixed up with other plants it doesn't work so easily.

The majority of our pots are made of terracotta. We also have some false lead containers, some old stone pots and troughs, and wooden boxes which our Head Gardener has made up from pallet deliveries. I try not to mix up the different types of material when displaying pots. While some plants such as solanum and agapanthus lend themselves to standing alone, or work as pairs on either side of seats or beside steps, others can be more effective grouped together.

PELARGONIUMS

There is a real problem with nomenclature when it comes to pelargoniums, which many people call geraniums. Apparently, Linnaeus originally grouped them together, but in 1789 Charles Louis L'Heritier de Brutelle separated them into two genera, though they are both part of the family *Geraniaceae*. The common name for pelargoniums is storkbills, and unless grown in sheltered town gardens in this country they need to be treated as tender perennials, whereas geraniums, commonly known as cranesbills, are hardy perennials. It is confusing when I am being asked to identify what visitors invariably name as a geranium until I realise they are actually talking about one of the pelargoniums, which form the

RIGHT ABOVE Pots of ivy leaf pelargoniums on wall of the south-west terrace
RIGHT BELOW Regal pelargoniums displayed on the Rose Garden terrace

main part of the tender plants in pots. Thank goodness for camera phones these days, so we can see a photo of one of our plants rather than receive a rather vague description of where they think they saw it in the garden! As we have such a large collection of different types of pelargonium, I will try and describe the different types below, along with other tender plants that we use.

Regal pelargoniums

The best examples of this group are displayed outside our garden room in the Rose Garden. They are in shades of either dark red and deep pink or white with dark red markings (dark red connects with plantings of *Rosa* 'Deep Secret' and *Antirrhinum* 'Black Prince' in the surrounding area). Two of the most popular regals are 'Lord Bute', which has dark red flowers with pale purple edges, and 'Cézanne', white with generous splashes of dark red and pink. The regal pelargoniums are usually the first to give a good show in early June, but in a normal British summer where we have a fair amount of rain, by late July their leaves tend to yellow while the flowers don't last and they need repatriating to the nursery area. However, as I am writing in the very hot summer of 2022, they are looking fantastic and have required only minimal deadheading even now in the middle of August. This group is probably the most spectacular amongst the pelargoniums we have, but they are averse to wet weather, so can require a lot of deadheading and defoliating.

Ivy leaf pelargoniums

This is another very popular group which also fares much better in a good summer and dislikes being wet. The colours range from dark red through many shades of pink to white, and they are best known for adorning balconies in Mediterranean countries where they flourish in the sunshine. There is, however, one in our collection which seems to be happy in the shade as well as the sun called 'Rose Silver Cascade'. This has a variegated leaf and deep pink flower and is very reliable. Another favourite is 'L'Élégante' with a slightly quieter variegated leaf and a white flower with deep pink marking. I particularly like the dark red 'Tommy' and a slightly lighter deep pink one called 'Simon Hornby'. If you are doing a mixed pot, these two go well with helichrysum foliage.

RIGHT (CLOCKWISE FROM TOP LEFT) *Pelargonium* 'Lord Bute'; *P.* 'Cézanne'; pots with *P.* 'Simon Hornby' and *Helichrysum petiolare*; *P.* 'L'Élégante'; *P.* 'Rose Silver Cascade'

Scented leaf pelargoniums

These are the ones which I like to place next to seats and on low walls so that people can touch them to appreciate their individual scent. This can range from rose to apple to mint to different spices and other delectable smells. The only trouble is that with only two hands it is impossible to compare more than two at a time! One of the most tactile of this group is *P. tomentosum*, which we plant up in the large copper on the left as you enter the garden. It has volumes of soft velvety leaves smelling of peppermint with tiny white flowers and is irresistible to passers-by. However, it dislikes being in full sunshine. Most scented leaf pelargoniums have unostentatious flowers and need sunshine, but there are a few exceptions in our collection: 'Clorinda' has fairly large, deep pink flowers and is very easy to manage; 'Purple Unique' has quite large purple flowers with beautiful large, soft green leaves; 'Copthorne' has masses of lilac flowers with purple markings, and 'Sweet Mimosa' has soft pink flowers. 'Mabel Grey' is renowned for its very powerful lemon scent, while the name 'Attar of Roses' speaks for itself. Two other old-fashioned favourites of mine are *P. fragrans* smelling of nutmeg and pine, and variegated 'Lady Plymouth' with a hint of rose and peppermint.

Species pelargoniums

The pelargonium which draws the most attention and elicits the most questions is a hybrid between *P. lobatum* and *P. fulgidum* called 'Ardens'. It has small, intensely red flowers with a darker red centre to each petal. This can be tricky both to propagate and to persuade into flower. We have moderate success in propagating it from heel cuttings, and I give it a really hard cut back in the early spring, reducing quite a number of the weird tubular roots and

chopping the top growth back hard before repotting in fresh compost. We have four pots of this pelargonium, which have now been flowering for twelve or more years – so far this rough treatment has not upset their performance. Generally, species pelargoniums are a disparate group, some of which are probably an acquired taste mainly appealing to collectors. However, there are several interesting ones such as the silver-leaf *P. sidoides* with small, intensely dark purple flowers, the coppery pink-flowered *P. friesdorf* and the unusual green-flowered *P. gibbosum*, to name just a few.

Other pelargoniums

This is a huge range and I will only name a few that we favour. 'Gazelle' has coral flowers and dark green leaves with zonal markings. It is totally reliable and a brilliant pelargonium which flowers all through the season. It is special because it was given to me by a good gardening friend, Janet Cropley, who has sadly since died, so it is a lovely reminder of her to have in the garden. There are several in the Unique group: 'Scarlet Unique' has a pure red flower perfectly set off by its soft green foliage; 'Crimson Unique' has larger deep pinkish red flowers with dark markings, and 'Paton's Unique' has deep pink flowers. These, together with 'Frank Headley', which has a variegated leaf with salmon flowers, are all inherited from my mother-in-law's collection. The rest are too many to name.

LEFT Scented leaf *Pelargonium tomentosum* (left) and *P.* 'Clorinda' (right)
ABOVE *Pelargonium* 'Ardens' (left) and *P.* 'Gazelle' (right)

OTHER PLANTS FOR CONTAINERS

Apart from pelargoniums we use ageratum, argyranthemum, convolvulus, diascia, species fuchsia, gazania, heliotrope, nemesia and osteospermum in pots. For foliage we make use of the silver and green forms of plectranthus, the architectural silver-leafed *Melianthus major*, plus the gold, silver and variegated forms of helichrysum. I make up just a few pots with mixed plantings. For example, I sometimes combine the purple *Heliotropium arborescens* with the gold form of helichrysum, or put together pink *Diascia* 'Apple Blossom' with blue *Convolvulus mauritanicus*. But I prefer to do single plantings.

The majority of pots are in sunny situations, either in the entrance and Stable Yard or on the terraces round the house. In the Gravel Garden we have a small collection of succulents in pots. In a slightly more formal way we put *Lilium regale* in pots, placed either side of the wellhead in the Italian Garden when they are in flower. On the south-east terrace we have a pair of a very pretty, delicate, white-flowered solanum shrubs in pots, and on the south-west terrace a pair of blue africanus agapanthus in wooden boxes at the top of the steps leading to the main lawn. At the far end of the Herb Garden there are a pair of pots with lemon verbena, *Aloysia citriodora*, either side of the seat for visitors to touch and enjoy their delicious lemon scent. In shady areas I use *Pelargonium tomentosum*, fuchsias, a foliage plant called *Rubus lineatus* with beautiful ribbed green leaves, and cultivars of hosta.

I have never really dared to count the number of pots of tender plants that we put out, but I think it is somewhere around 150. I am often asked how we cope with watering and feeding so many pots. I am very grateful to my husband, Ian, who undertakes the almost daily watering of those pots in the garden during the main summer months. It takes him a good hour in the evening or early morning. We do not actually feed the pots when they are out. They are planted each year in the compost which we use for all the plants that we sell from the nursery. This is a mixture of peat-free compost with grit, which also contains granules of slow-release Osmocote fertiliser.

At the end of the season all the pots are transported to the Stable Yard, where we are able to cover them with fleece in the event of an early frost. Final cuttings are taken before the plants are cut back roughly by half in order to squeeze them into the polytunnel. In late winter and early spring on wet or frozen days when we are unable to work in the garden, we start the process of going through all the pots, emptying them, removing old compost, trimming back the top growth, reducing the roots and repotting them in fresh compost. Before replanting, we soak the rootball rather than water the pot, as most of them only need a small amount of water in the winter months. Most of the plants, particularly the pelargoniums, will be reused, but every so often we need to replace some, and on the whole I prefer to start a pot with completely

ABOVE LEFT *Verbena* 'Silver Anne' and *Helichrysum petiolare*
ABOVE RIGHT *Fuchsia* 'Chequerboard'
LEFT *Heliotropium arborescens* and *Clematis* 'Jackmanii Superba'

new plants if we have them available rather than mix old and new. From late April onwards, we start to move some pots outside the polytunnel, but the majority do not go out into the garden until late May and the beginning of June.

TROUGHS

There is a stone trough just before the door that leads into the garden which contains hardy plants. As it faces north-west and doesn't receive much sun, it has plants that can cope with shade. These include *Helleborus* 'Magic Leaves'; the early white-flowering *Iberis sempervirens*; the maidenhair fern, *Adiantum venustum*; the broad buckler fern, *Dryopteris austriaca* 'Lepidota Cristata'; *Parahebe* 'Snow Clouds'; pink-flowered *Crassula sarcocaulis* and *Fuchsia magellanica* 'Hawkshead' with dainty white flowers. They provide quiet interest throughout the year, and I have deliberately chosen plants with different foliage and delicate flowers to create contrasting texture.

As I mentioned earlier, alpine gardening is not something I have a passion for, but I do like having a few sinks on the terraces where we can display these types of plants and their detail

can be appreciated. Succulents are perfect candidates for this sunny situation, and we have a number of different alpine sedums and sempervivums. Surprisingly, the delightful alpine *Phlox divaricata* subsp. *laphamii* 'Chattahoochee', with its blue, purple-centred flowers, flourishes in these sinks despite the very shallow depth of soil. Also planted here are the silver *Artemisia schmidtiana* 'Nana', the miniature *Leucojum autumnale*, *Erodium guttatum* and *E. chrysanthum*, *Sisyrinchium* 'E. K. Balls', smaller forms of dianthus and small-leaf thymes. In sinks with a little more depth we have included the silver foliage plant *Convolvulus cneorum*, the dark-leaf *Heuchera* 'Obsidian', *Helianthemum* 'Lawrenson's Pink', the harebell *Campanula rotundifolia* and *Potentilla* 'White Queen'. However, this is not a complete list, and we do vary the planting here from time to time.

LEFT *Agapanthus africanus* and *Lotus berthelotii* at the top of the rill
ABOVE A sink containing alpines beneath *Rosa multiflora* 'Platyphylla' (Seven Sisters' rose) and surrounded by *Centranthus ruber* on the south-west terrace

Wildflower Areas

GENERALLY SPEAKING, the comments we hear most frequently from visitors refer to the peace, tranquillity and restfulness they find in the garden, and many say how therapeutic it is for them. As the gardener, that is music to my ears, and it always pleases me to know that the aura of the garden is reaching people on a level beyond just the visual effect. Although it has a reputation for colourful borders, there are many areas where the planting is more subdued and seats where people can sit and contemplate. However, there are three areas – one within the garden and two beyond it – dedicated to wildflowers and their relatives. From a flowering point of view, all of them perform in spring and early summer, although the wood, to my mind, is just as enchanting with or without bluebells.

While the bluebells in the wood were already established, we started planting the early spring-flowering meadow in the Old Orchards shortly after we took over the garden, and the creation of the Wildflower Meadow in the field beyond the garden, adjacent to the Bluebell Wood, was begun in 1994. I like to think these areas both within and beyond the garden exude a degree of informality which blends with the lower parts of the garden and the surrounding countryside.

THE OLD ORCHARDS

Having dismantled the wire surrounding the orchards which hitherto had contained my father-in-law's rather fierce emperor geese, we were left with two ponds which he had created for them. After a few years we decided there was

The Old Orchards in spring

no point to the ponds, and at this juncture asked Head Gardener Richard Green if he could divert the spring-fed pond water to create a rill running between the two orchards. With great ingenuity he managed to carry out this not insignificant challenge, using just enough water for the rill without diminishing the flow through the Water Garden. Initially, we planted four groups of snowdrops (*Galanthus nivalis*), which have been added to over the years and now provide sheets of white flowers in late winter and early spring. These are followed by *Crocus tommasinianus*, which has naturalised to create patches of purple overlapping with the snowdrops. To our delight, we have also managed to naturalise both the purple and white forms of snakeshead fritillary, *Fritillaria meleagris*, which flower alongside early forms of narcissus. Then there are cowslips, *Primula veris*, and the silver and white flowers of *Ornithogalum nutans*. By May, under a canopy of pear and apple blossom, groups of pheasant's eye narcissus, *N. poeticus*, and blue *Camassia quamash* decorate the ground below. At this stage ox-eye daisies, *Leucanthemum vulgare*, have somehow managed to add themselves into the mix, and it is always a rather sad moment when eventually the grass needs to be cut around the end of June and the last of the flowers disappear.

Over the years we have introduced quite a few roses into the orchards. A group of three *Rosa* 'Nevada' are the first to flower, and their lovely semi-double white flowers look completely natural in this grassy area. Higher up on the other side of the rill we have more recently planted a group of three 'Marguerite Hilling', a pink sport of 'Nevada'. Elsewhere is the double white, green-centred 'Madame Hardy', which we have tried to form into a spider shape by bending the stems down on to hazel supports to create more flowers from its long stems. In the opposite orchard we have applied the same technique to 'Constance Spry', also renowned for producing long stems. 'Climbing Cécile Brünner' used to wind up into one of the fruit trees until the tree died, when we managed to resurrect a fallen tree trunk from elsewhere, up which it happily rewound itself. Up another fruit tree clambers the small double-flowered 'Chevy Chase', whose lovely deep crimson flowers appearing over the top of the tree are clearly visible from the

LEFT *Crocus tommasinianus* and *Galanthus nivalis* in the Old Orchards in early spring
ABOVE *Fritillaria meleagris* and *Primula veris* in the Old Orchards in spring

adjacent Goose Park area of the garden. 'Brewood Belle' spreads its strong pink flowers over the trunk of an apple tree, flowering through most of the summer. But the star of the show here was 'Francis E. Lester', which I planted to grow over and light up a large holly bush on one side of the orchard, only to find two years later that it had reached above the holly to climb into a very tall silver birch. The masses of its pink-tinged white flowers provide a wonderful display in July for people looking down the Water Garden towards the summer house, and indeed it can also be seen from the lawn terrace above the pond. However, apart from its trunk, it is no longer visible in the orchard. Both 'Nevada' and 'Marguerite Hilling' put on a second show of flowers. But in the autumn, apart from the apples and pears decorating the trees, it is left to a few patches of the autumn-flowering *Crocus speciosus* 'Oxonian' to put on a display.

We had a curved bench made for the bottom of the orchards so that visitors could sit and enjoy looking at the view uphill, watching our flock of bantams pecking the ground in search

Rosa 'Nevada' flowering in the Old Orchards in May

of worms and listening to the sound of the water dropping down the rill. It is rewarding to see how frequently it is occupied. It feels like the heart of the garden here, and it is reassuring to be able to see the gables of the house from this vantage point – so not too far for that cup of tea!

THE BLUEBELL WOOD

A gate at the bottom right-hand corner of the garden leads into the Wildflower Meadow and also to the Bluebell Wood. The wood is usually in full flower from about the third week of April and for the first ten days of May, but the dates are unpredictable, depending on whether we have had an early or late spring. The flowering time is good because it overlaps with the later performance in the orchards. Likewise, as the bluebells (*Hyacinthoides non-scripta*) fade, so buttercups (*Ranunculus acris*) are starting to flower in the adjacent meadow.

For some years, somewhat to my frustration, Coton was more renowned for its bluebell wood than its garden. For many visitors it was an annual pilgrimage. We don't know how long the bluebells have been in the wood, although Ian's uncle remembered them flowering when his parents first bought Coton in the 1920s. But since it is ancient woodland (marked as Coton Park) on old maps, it is likely that they go back a long way. We think, but cannot be sure, that the beech trees must have been added in the 1920s by my husband's grandparents, partly due to their age and partly because we have been told that beech is not a native Northamptonshire tree. There are also a lot of beech trees in the garden, so that generation was probably responsible for introducing them here.

The wood is completely magical at any time of year, but particularly so at bluebell time. As you enter, the colour of the flowers seems at its most intense and their fragrance likewise. The vertical trunks of the beech trees create an almost cathedral-like effect, enhanced by the wood being on a rake uphill. There is virtually no middle storey planting – just the odd holly bush – and since it is only 2 ha/5 acres and surrounded by farmland it is not dark. Many people comment on the spiritual feeling they experience when visiting the wood, and that is something I share with them.

When we took over the garden in 1991, bluebells completely covered the floor of the wood and remained like that for fifteen years or so. But very gradually, they have been fading on the south-west side, and this loss has now become quite pronounced. Initially, we thought it might be because of the crop in the adjacent field being sprayed. But with the introduction of a crop of miscanthus many years ago, there was no further need for fertilisers or pesticides, so that was obviously not the cause. We do have muntjac deer in the wood, but they don't seem to dig up the bluebells, nor is there any evidence of other animals digging them. The only cause we can think of is the south-west wind which hits that side of the wood and has definitely increased in strength over the years. There is clear evidence that the leaf mould gets blown across the wood and that the coverage is quite thin where the bluebells are struggling. We have tried adding our own

garden compost to improve the mulching, but it doesn't appear to make any difference. Also, I know from my experience in the garden that bluebells are thugs and will prosper anywhere if we don't halt them. To dig them up you have to go very deep with a fork. So we are somewhat bewildered about how to try and redress the problem.

The wood still looks wonderful in late April and early May with the lime green foliage of the beech trees just emerging and providing a perfect backdrop for the bluebells below. When the sun shines through the trees, it is indeed a magical sight, and it is lovely that so many people are able to enjoy it as bluebell woods are not as abundant as they were in my childhood. Ironically, as I write during the exceptional summer of 2022, the wood has had many visitors throughout the summer months because it is wonderfully cool on a hot day and also immensely peaceful.

THE WILDFLOWER MEADOW

One of the reasons we decided to create a wildflower meadow beyond the garden was because after the crop in the field had been harvested, we found there was suddenly an area of brown soil where the garden ended rather abruptly. Also, I knew that Richard, our gardener, was very keen on the idea. So in 1994 we embarked on making the Wildflower Meadow in the remaining part of the field, the other half of which had been taken into the garden in the late 1960s. I seem to recall that we scattered some wildflower seeds in concentrated areas to start with, and a path was mown for visitors to walk through it.

But however lovely it was to walk through waving grasses, it was almost impossible to discern any wildflowers until one day a kindly visitor suggested that we should sow yellow rattle seeds, *Rhinanthus minor*, a parasitic annual which feeds on the stronger grasses. This we proceeded to do,

The Bluebell Wood in early May

initially with rather disappointing results. But after a year or two of persuading everyone to go out and collect the rattle seed which we then scattered far and wide, this finally began to yield positive results. During this period Richard had also grown quite a number of wildflowers from seed into plugs which were then planted out, and they gradually started to increase while at the same time the stronger grasses receded. It is all a question of balance. Over the years we have had to try and cut the meadow towards the end of July before the knapweed, *Centaurea nigra*, scatters its seeds and becomes too dominant.

The meadow starts off with a sea of dandelions, which is a very cheering sight in late April, and is then followed by sheets of meadow buttercups, *Ranunculus acris*. Originally, the dominant plants thereafter were ox-eye daisies, *Leucanthemum vulgare*. But that has changed over the years, and now they are just part of a mix of other wildflowers such as the blue meadow cranesbill (*Geranium pratense*), ragged robin (*Lychnis flos-cuculi*), red and white clover (*Trifolium pratense*), meadow vetching (*Lathyrus pratensis*), devil's bit scabious (*Succisa pratensis*), hawkbit (*Leontodon hispidus*), sheep's sorrel (*Rumex acetosella*), selfheal (*Prunella vulgaris*), bird's foot trefoil (*Lotus corniculatus*), common vetch (*Vicia sativa*), tufted vetch (*Vicia cracca*), plus many

more and a variety of the more delicate grasses – too many to name here. For those who visit the garden to see the meadow in flower, it starts towards the end of May and continues until it is cut towards the end of July. There is a display board by the gate through which you pass to enter the meadow which describes the various flowers and grasses you may find.

I know the meadow gives a lot of pleasure to many visitors and indeed to ourselves, and I am really grateful to Richard Green for managing it so beautifully. After the garden closes at the end of September, he allows our small herd of Longhorn cattle to come into the meadow for a few weeks to both eat down the grass and tread in the seed. After that it is left until the spring when the path is remown, and it is opened to visitors just as the Bluebell Wood finishes flowering.

LEFT The Wildflower Meadow with *Ranunculus acris* (meadow buttercups) in late May
ABOVE *Geranium pratense* (cranesbill), *Vicia cracca* (tufted vetch) and *Centaurea nigra* (lesser knapweed) in July
OVERLEAF The Wildflower Meadow in late June with *Leucanthemum vulgare* (ox-eye daisies)

Scent in the Garden

O NE OF THE GREATEST PLEASURES as I wander around a garden is a heightened sense of smell. Simple ones like the smell that follows a shower of rain, the first time the grass is cut in spring, walking through the orchards at blossom time or a bonfire in winter resonate as well as the more specific scents of flowers or the aroma of herbs when touched. Some smells are evocative and immediately take me back in time. Others are just a surprise and delight: for example, digging in the borders in the depths of winter and suddenly coming across a delicious whiff of monarda – an unusual plant in that every part of it, including the roots, has a distinctive bergamot smell which always stops me in my tracks and makes me smile. However, a sense of smell – rather like taste – is subjective, and it is hard to imagine living without it, which a number of people suffering from anosmia do. Meanwhile, there are some scents or smells we are unable to detect while others can and other odours we may not like but others do. For instance, much to my frustration, I can never pick up what I am told is the caramel or burnt toffee smell given off by the katsura tree, *Cercidiphyllum japonicum*, in late summer, and while others seem to enjoy the scent of *Trachelospermum asiaticum* just inside the entrance to the garden, it doesn't appeal to me. Scents can be elusive inasmuch as they can vary in strength according to the weather, the time of day and the seasons.

I think it is always worth considering where to place any scented plant so that it can be appreciated by passers-by. Where possible I enjoy having scented plants by doorways or where people have to pass through narrow spaces, although many plants do require you to bend down to pick up their fragrance – a familiar sight in our garden.

I believe that the terraces on the south-west and south-east sides of the house have always been planted with scent in mind and that remains the case today. The idea is that these scents should occur gradually so that there is a succession of smells rather than too many overlapping ones. The scent season on the first terrace commences with *Osmanthus delavayi*, which is reputed to have a delicate smell but I am afraid it eludes me; the next plant which does have a very strong fragrance is the dwarf lilac, *Syringa meyeri* 'Palibin', which when in flower scents the whole terrace. This is followed by three *Rosa multiflora* 'Platyphylla' (Seven Sisters' rose) on the

RIGHT ABOVE Primroses and violets in the Woodland Garden
RIGHT BELOW *Agastache foeniculum* (anise hyssop) and *Hedychium* 'Assam Orange' (ginger plant)

house walls, which between them provide a good month of sweetly scented flowers, after which there is *Trachelospermum asiaticum* and finally, by September, the pale yellow cowslip-scented flowers of *Clematis rehderiana*. At a lower level throughout the main part of summer there are plants in pots, particularly *Heliotropium arborescens* (known as 'cherry pie') and several scented leaf pelargoniums which need to be touched to reveal their various aromas.

Coming round the corner of the house in May, you would have been overwhelmed by a waft of perfume from the wisteria which sadly is no more, having died in 2022 after, we suspect, about one hundred years. However, there is another wisteria on this side of the house that can still be enjoyed. In late April *Viburnum carlesii* exudes one of the strongest perfumes in the garden, which I would like to distil and bottle, and later there are a number of sweetly smelling roses and more scented leaf pelargoniums to be touched. In a pot on the terrace there is an unusual plant called *Sinningia tubiflora* with white flowers which have a delicious scent. And on the next terrace outside our garden room in summer there are more roses, the confederate jasmine, *Trachelospermum jasminoides*, a scented clematis called *C. odorata*, which in addition to its attractive small purple flowers produces a mass of pretty seed heads, and a large myrtle (*Myrtus communis*) with aromatic leaves and fluffy white flowers in late summer.

There have been many books written about scent in the garden, and what follows will only scratch the surface of this subject. I am just going to provide a rough calendar guide in terms of timing as we move through the seasons of those that I personally enjoy. I will start with winter because although the flowers on winter-flowering shrubs may not be large and spectacular,

ABOVE *Mahonia × media* 'Charity' (left) and *Daphne bholua* 'Jacqueline Postill' (right)
RIGHT *Viburnum carlesii* (left) and *Convallaria majalis* (right)

they do produce some of the strongest and sweetest scents as they attempt to attract insects for pollination, and most of them have a generously long flowering period.

There is very little in flower in the garden in November, which strictly speaking is still part of autumn, but *Mahonia × media* 'Charity' does produce very fragrant yellow flowers reminiscent of the scent of lily of the valley (*Convallaria majalis*). If you reduce some of the holly-like leaves, it is a lovely thing to bring into the house at this rather bleak time of year. A bit further into winter there are several forms of sarcococca which have very small but strongly scented white flowers. It is the sort of scent which can be carried on the air for quite a distance around the shrub, and I find myself smiling involuntarily each time I pick it up – one of the true bonuses of winter. We have many different species round the garden, but the one which I find has the strongest scent is *S. ruscifolia*, and this is the one I tend to pick to take inside the house. At some point in January our *Daphne bholua* 'Jacqueline Postill' starts flowering. This shrub is really worth having because it produces pretty deep pink buds which open into intensely fragrant white flowers that continue well into March. Unlike other daphnes which I have tried growing, it is totally straightforward and hardy; it even produces occasional suckers which can be potted up and eventually planted out elsewhere. *Lonicera fragrantissima* is another winter-flowering shrub with very strongly scented white flowers, likewise *Viburnum × bodnantense* 'Dawn', which has clusters of sweetly scented pink flowers.

In March and April the woodland violet, *Viola odorata*, renowned for its scent is a delight as it scrambles amongst exposed tree roots, likewise the pink flowers of *V. odorata* 'Coeur d'Alsace', along with the delicate scents of primulas and narcissus – the most scented form being the pheasant's eye *Narcissus poeticus*, which doesn't usually flower here until May. In the Stable Yard there is a vigorous climber, *Akebia quinata*, known as the chocolate vine, growing on the side of the restaurant. This vine has clusters of pretty dark red flowers with a faint smell of vanilla in April.

It is hard to know when summer starts as it can be so variable depending on the weather, but for me the distinctive smell of lupins and iris heralds the onset of summer and I really love that moment and those flowers. Also at this stage there is a plethora of scented plants emerging in different parts of the garden, such as lily of the valley, *Convallaria majalis*, and *Smilacina racemosa*, both with their gloriously scented white flowers in the Woodland Garden, together with different forms of the delicately scented *Viola cornuta* spread round shadier areas. The scent of the yellow azalea, *Rhododendron lutea*, permeates the whole of the Water Garden in May – one of early summer's most evocative smells; yellow-flowered *Ribes odorata* is well named; the tiny yellow flowers of the silver-leaf *Elaeagnus* 'Quicksilver' produce a surprisingly sweet scent; there are several more specimens of the highly scented lilac *Syringa meyeri* 'Palibin' in sunnier areas, while different forms of tree peony (particularly *Paeonia delavayi* and *P. delavayi* × (× *suffruticosa*)) that beguile us with their exotic flowers also delight with their particular fragrance. But the outstanding sensory experience in this garden in May is walking into and around the Bluebell Wood – a treat for the eyes, the nose and the soul.

As we move into summer there are perhaps too many scented plants to enumerate, but herbaceous peonies (*Paeonia lactiflora*), sweet peas (*Lathyrus odoratus*), pinks (dianthus), sweet rocket (*Hesperis matronalis*), honeysuckle (lonicera) and mock orange (philadelphus) are all evocative of that moment when there is a sudden burst of flowering and it's hard to keep up with everything that is performing. For me, amongst everything else the undoubted winners in this contest are the many roses. The first to flower in late May with a very pronounced scent is

ABOVE *Syringa meyeri* 'Palibin' (left) and *Rosa* 'Mme Isaac Pereire' (right)
RIGHT *Phlox* × *arendsii* 'Luc's Lilac' (left) and *Magnolia grandiflora* (right)

a rugosa which I inherited from my mother-in-law called *Rosa* 'Belle Poitevine'. It has beautiful double pink flowers and literally flowers all summer at the top of the Rose Bank. After that there is a succession of roses flowering until the first frost. I have lost track of how many we have in the garden, but I know from June onwards that there is always another within reach to enjoy. If I am pushed to name my favourite scented roses, I would probably mention 'Étoile de Hollande', 'Mme Isaac Pereire', 'Lady Emma Hamilton', 'Autumn Sunset', 'Louise Odier', 'Gertrude Jekyll', 'Constance Spry', *R. multiflora* 'Platyphylla' (Seven Sisters' rose) and 'Ghislaine de Féligonde'. Nothing else in the garden can compete with this avalanche of scent from one genus.

Slightly later in summer there is scent to be found in border phlox, monarda, galtonia, agastache, herbaceous clematis, crinum, nicotianas and the climbers *Trachelospermum asiaticum* and *T. jasminoides*, *Hedychium* 'Assam Orange', and in the particularly heady perfume of various lilies and *Magnolia grandiflora*. Both the pale blue *Clematis* 'Betty Corning', which is beside the ramp leading up to the main yard, and the late flowering pale yellow *C. rehderiana* by the door as you enter the garden have a delicate scent which can be picked up in passing.

Finally, there is another group of plants which yield a more aromatic rather than a sweet smell and which need to be touched in order for it to be released. This includes the many herbs such as rosemary, bay, thyme, sage, lavender, fennel, hyssop, sweet cicely and lemon verbena – all of which can be found in our Herb Garden, in the middle of which is a sundial surrounded by chamomile. This is deliberately here so that on a sunny day it can be trodden on by those attempting to read the time, releasing the plant's unique smell. As mentioned above, the many scented leaf forms of pelargonium also fall into this group that needs to be touched. I think that writing about scented plants has made me conscious of the fact that I lack the vocabulary to accurately describe the myriad different smells given off by plants, and I can only suggest that 'sniffing plant perfumes' is one of the most uplifting experiences to be enjoyed in the garden.

Wildlife and Sculpture

I T MAY SEEM SOMEWHAT BIZARRE to group these two aspects together, but it is because there is sometimes a confusion between them. At a certain point when visitors are in the lower part of the garden walking along the path that divides the Rose Bank from the Midsummer Border, they spot the sculpture of a stag in the Wildflower Meadow beyond; I not infrequently hear people exclaim, assuming that it is alive until they realise that it isn't moving. Quite often looking in the same direction but within the garden people can see our flamingos, which have a habit of standing motionless, and they in turn are often assumed to be sculptures. It is what you might describe as a rather charming but totally uncontrived conceit.

WILDLIFE

During my parents-in-law's time, the garden was actually known as Coton Manor Wildlife Garden due to the number of exotic birds and waterfowl which my father-in-law had introduced, including at one point two sea lions and later some penguins. By the time we took on the garden, the majority of his collection had been reduced to a few pheasants, peacocks, cranes, geese, ducks and flamingos, but we were left with quite an expanse of aviary, cages and wired off areas which we gradually dismantled. The pheasants, peacocks and geese were given away while we retained the flamingos, ducks and cranes, all of which could roam free in the garden, until unfortunately the cranes were killed by a fox some years ago. I think it is fair to say that nowadays this is neither a wildlife nor a sculpture garden, but we do retain elements of both.

Flamingos are obviously an unusual bird to find in an English garden. The original group of twelve were acquired by my father-in-law in the early 1970s, three of which we still have. And we recently added four younger ones. The deep pink birds originate in the Caribbean and the paler ones come from Africa. They are all given the same prepared food, which contains the necessary ingredients to help retain their colour. They remain outside throughout the year and cannot be persuaded to go under cover, even in ice or snow. Having seen a television programme on flamingos in Tierra del Fuego a while ago where the birds become frozen into the water overnight

RIGHT ABOVE The Meadow Border in October with flamingos in the foreground and cows eating the grass down in the Wildflower Meadow beyond
RIGHT BELOW Sculpture of the stag in the Wildflower Meadow.

and have to wait until the sun melts the ice the following morning before they are able to move, we are no longer quite as concerned as we used to be about protecting them in our relatively mild winters. They are amazingly unfazed by people in the garden and often give the impression of posing for photographs. They make use of the different water areas, although they spend most of their time in the lower parts. They are remarkably little trouble and give us all so much pleasure.

In the lower orchard beyond the area open to visitors, we have a number of laying hens and bantams, while running round the lower part of the garden like a group of naughty schoolchildren is a flock of Mille Fleur Barbu d'Uccle bantams which cause a lot of amusement. They are very colourful and look for all the world like moving plants. They can often be spotted bedecking one of the seats intended for visitors. They do a certain amount of unwarranted 'gardening' in some of the borders, but they are so much part of the place that we have learnt to live with them over the years, and for the most part they aren't too much of a problem.

Our collection of ducks fluctuates according to how successfully we manage to intervene by finding the nests of those we wish to breed from and rescuing the eggs to put in the incubator and hopefully hatch. Ducks are notoriously bad parents, and left to their own devices the ducklings are lucky to survive. Our favourite breed is a tree duck called fulvous whistling. They stand higher than other ducks, are light brown with darker brown markings, and they whistle to each other when they become separated. They are enchanting and amuse us by following each other around the garden in single file. There are also mandarins, Carolinas, Chiloé wigeons and teal, plus visiting mallards and moorhens at large in the garden.

Moving away from feathered varieties, we have a very small herd of Longhorn cattle numbering around twelve. They are easily identifiable with their spectacular horns, often in somewhat erratic shapes, and are generally peaceful and great to behold in the surrounding fields. We usually have three or four calves a year. They produce the most excellent quality meat, although as a family we are not huge meat eaters, so we sell it and use it for the excellent lasagne which is made in the cafe kitchen.

Finally, in this somewhat idiosyncratic collection of birds and animals, we have three Kunekune pigs, a New Zealand rare breed, which are hugely popular. They are so friendly and responsive to people who visit them in their pen at the end of the Woodland Garden and are particularly appealing to small children. And, no, we do not breed them to be eaten – they are just here to be enjoyed.

RIGHT (CLOCKWISE FROM TOP LEFT) Bantams commandeering a seat; fulvous whistling ducks in single file; Kunekune pigs; bees at work on an echinops; tortoiseshell butterfly alighting on an aster; longhorn cows

In a more natural way we are also home to numerous bees, hoverflies, butterflies and occasional hummingbird hawkmoths. These insects really do provide an extra dimension of pleasure for all those observant enough to enjoy them, especially in the later summer months. I am often asked which plants they most enjoy, and I would say that on the whole it is the later flowering plants to which bees seem to be attracted, particularly any plants related to the veronica family, together with salvias, monardas and sedums. Earlier in summer they are also busy in the Wildflower Meadow. We also spot the occasional water vole, hedgehog and toad, the last being somewhat hazardous when we are forking the borders.

SCULPTURE

We didn't inherit any straightforward sculpture in the garden, but both previous generations of the family did install some beautiful pieces of stonework in varied locations. There are two attractive fountains with cherubs spouting water. The first one is seen on your right as you enter the garden, and the second one is in the Rose Garden facing the garden room. There are also two wellheads – one that my father-in-law acquired from Crowthers in London which sits in what they named the Italian Garden at the foot of the main lawn and the other in the centre of the quartered circle in the Rose Garden. This one we believe to be a nineteenth- or early twentieth-century copy of an early Renaissance Florentine wellhead with designs from the Cantoria by Luca della Robbia. There are also stone pots (some on pedestals), obelisks and tables in different places and stone ornaments at various points around the main pond. In their understated way these pieces give the garden a sense of age and permanence, and we are grateful for their vision in selecting and placing them so effectively.

Over the years we have added a few pieces of sculpture. The garden is not formal and it doesn't major on focal points, so the artefacts we have added are quite varied and hopefully in keeping with its feeling of informality. I think the first one we acquired was a Haddonstone sculpture of Venus which is a copy of a late nineteenth-century Italian sculpture. We first sited this in what we called the Statue Bed within the Woodland Garden, but she never looked very comfortable there. We then placed her in the Gravel Garden, where she is situated at one rocky corner with water trickling round her. It is quite extraordinary how much more appropriate she seems in this position, both in scale and surroundings. I think placing sculpture in the right position within a

RIGHT (CLOCKWISE FROM TOP LEFT) Nineteenth-century copy of Renaissance Florentine wellhead, planted with *Tulipa* 'Exotic Emperor'; cherub fountain at the entrance to the south-west terrace; Haddonstone sculpture of Venus in the Gravel Garden; second cherub fountain in the Rose Garden

garden context is quite challenging. In the Statue Bed we replaced Venus with a charming sculpture made by Mary Cox of Pan playing his pipes. Elsewhere we had placed a small sculpture of two frogs on a lily pad in a small pond at the end of the Canal Run, where it was quite exposed and never felt right. Recently, we moved the frogs to a smaller pool in the Dells under some trees, and they look completely perfect. In the Water Garden, as you emerge from the privet tunnel, almost hidden by rhododendrons is a small sculpture of a fawn sitting on a log playing a pipe. The idea is that it might stop children in their tracks as they rush down the tunnel, and I think sometimes it does.

On a larger scale, for his seventieth birthday I gave my husband a sculpture of a stag made by George Hider which we had seen exhibited on a visit to Cothay Gardens in Somerset. He has perfected the art of constructing animals from scrap steel and manages to make his sculptures look amazingly real. We have sited the stag in the Wildflower Meadow close to the Bluebell Wood, so that it looks as if it has just emerged from the wood and has been startled by something. This is so effective that, as I have mentioned above, this works on more than one level, both persuading people from a distance that it is alive and also delighting those who find themselves close to it as they walk the path round the meadow. Our most recent acquisition was a bronze mantle

made by David Harber which we bought to celebrate our fiftieth wedding anniversary. This has been an outstanding success. It is a delicate latticework of verdigris bronze petals, the underside gilded with gold leaf. Everybody assumes that it is lit, but it is merely the reflection of the gold leaf, which is slightly more obvious on dull days. We have positioned it in a small pool, and it can only be seen as you emerge through the archway leading into the Woodland Garden from the Rose Garden. The comparative coolness and green-ness of this area is in complete contrast to the relatively formal, colourful and sunny rose garden, and I like to feel that the ethereal glow of the mantle is in harmony with the calmer mood of this woodland glade. In the autumn the leaves from a Norway maple fall into the water and they reflect the shape of the latticework of the sculpture, which makes it even more effective. It certainly causes huge interest, and despite the lapse of time since it was installed, it never fails to delight me as I walk past it.

LEFT Frogs on a lily pad in a pool in the Dells
ABOVE Bronze mantle by David Harber in the Woodland Garden

A Reason to Smile

ON THE WHOLE I would say that gardeners are quite serious and thoughtful people, but there are so many moments in the garden when I find myself smiling involuntarily with delight, and it is perhaps this feeling which has prompted me to write about my experiences in the hope that it might encourage others to discover for themselves the pleasure gardening can provide. The following paragraphs describe just a few of these random moments.

So often it is what nature does for us without prompting that brings a smile. An unusually beautiful pink hellebore that has seeded itself into the stone wall below the main hellebore bed – an impossible place to plant, but so effective. Or the winter-flowering *Helleborus foetidus* which positioned itself beside the gravel path, where its lime green flowers rimmed with red are highlighted against a yew hedge; the magenta-flowered *Geranium palmatum* with its fresh green foliage growing in a bed backed by a stone wall, managing to seed itself in two places at the top of the wall; the ostrich fern, *Matteuccia struthiopteris*, unfurling in spring; the pleasure of seeing butterflies perching on the cone of a helenium flower or atop a kniphofia, several butterflies sharing an escallonia bush; bees feeding on the lavender hedge in the Rose Garden and on sedums, echinops and echinaceas. In winter the sunsets frequently stop me in my tracks and cause me to smile because they are so bewitchingly beautiful and never the same.

Then there are the effects which have been planned and prove to work. I am constantly trying to organize colours that I hope will work together, and it is very rewarding when they do. In the Rose Garden towards the end of the season *Acidanthera bicolor* is planted next to the dark red *Rosa* 'Deep Secret', the dark red centre of the gladiolus echoing the colour of the rose; the harmony of *Clematis viticella* 'Madame Julia Correvon' threading its way through *Rosa multiflora* 'Platyphylla' (Seven Sisters' rose) on the house wall; the contrast of purple *C.* 'Jackmanii Superba' planted against the apricot shades of *R.* 'Ghislaine de Féligonde', to mention just a few.

RIGHT (CLOCKWISE FROM TOP LEFT) *Helleborus foetidus* flowering in February; *Matteucia struthiopteris* (ostrich fern) with leaves unfurling in spring; *C. cirrhosa* 'Freckles'; butterfly atop a helenium; *Tulipa batalinii* 'Bronze Charm'; *Rosa* 'Ghislaine de Féligonde' and *Clematis* 'Jackmanii Superba'

A few years ago I had a winter-flowering *Clematis cirrhosa* 'Freckles' growing in a shady corner of the Rose Garden, where it didn't seem to be very happy, so I moved it to what I hoped was a better situation in our entrance yard where it didn't flourish either. So, finally I moved it again to grow up a silver birch tree at the entrance to the Bog Garden. It took at least a couple of years to start growing more of its glossy evergreen foliage, and then suddenly recently it has produced a generous amount of its exquisite flowers, which are nodding bell shapes with deep pink markings on the inside of the petals. In its third location we are able to look up and appreciate the full beauty of the flowers, and it is hard to describe how much pleasure that has given me. I visit it nearly every day when it is flowering to enjoy the spectacle, and it does so for a long time between December and February. It is precisely this typical garden experience of trial and error, if and when it eventually works, that causes me to smile.

A problem with *Romneya coulteri*, the Californian tree poppy, was another instance. For several years we attempted unsuccessfully to establish this in perhaps too shady a spot at the top of our Mediterranean Bank, and finally we moved it to a sunny position at the back of the Acacia Border where it has more space, and now in its second summer, much to our surprise and delight, it is flourishing and producing masses of the poached egg-like flowers for which it is renowned.

I find that twelve months is just long enough for me to forget some things I have planted, and it is always a thrill seeing plants which I had put in with considerable thought and care the previous season – and had temporarily forgotten – coming into flower. That definitely induces a smile, and reminds me of the importance of labelling. A few years ago I noticed a particularly beautiful small tulip growing on a narrow raised ledge in the Water Garden which I subsequently discovered my wonderful gardener Sue had planted as a surprise birthday present for me. It is *Tulipa batalinii* 'Bronze Charm' in shades of soft apricot-orange and, being a species tulip, it appears every year in slightly increasing numbers. Each year it is still a lovely surprise. I think the same goes for *Cyclamen hederifolium*, which is dormant through late spring and early summer; suddenly in late July the flowers start to appear and it is always an unexpected delight to see them.

Over the course of three decades I have had numerous plants given to me by generous friends. I never forget the kind people who provided them, and it is a pleasure to walk past and recall where a particular plant came from. This always causes me to remember that person, some of whom are no longer around, and the reminder brings a smile to my face.

Birdsong always lifts my spirits, although I have to admit that I am not very good at identifying which bird's song I am listening to. But there is one that is very familiar. The robin is constantly with us when we are gardening in winter, singing away and quite intrepid when seizing a worm close to our forks and spades. Its presence always makes us smile, especially when it is trying to see off another robin from what it regards as its territory or perching on top of a spade, reminiscent of a scene from Frances Hodgson Burnett's *The Secret Garden*.

I love the scents of flowers. It is curious how subjective smells can be. As I have remarked, I find it deeply frustrating that (unlike almost everybody else) I am unable to detect what I am told is the smell of caramel released around the katsura tree, *Cercidiphyllum japonicum*. Equally, I can pick up the scent of the pale blue *Clematis* 'Betty Corning', which grows along the wall leading up to the garden door into the yard, and I have yet to find many others who can smell it. Putting one's face into one of those huge *Magnolia grandiflora* flowers is an extraordinary sensory experience – to my nose like a very heady gardenia. I can seldom resist smelling roses as I am deadheading or picking them, and they all have distinctively different scents. I always think the smell of irises and lupins heralds the start of summer, which is a lovely moment to reach in the garden. We have a large collection of scented leaf pelargoniums, and I like to place pots beside seats so that people can stroke them and enjoy their scent, which is something I frequently do myself on passing.

One of my favourite jobs is pruning roses, particularly climbing roses which need to be bent horizontally to maximize their flowering potential. Sometimes it can be daunting to know where to begin when looking at a rose on a frame that has become overgrown during the previous season. But it is somewhat akin to doing a jigsaw puzzle, working out which stems should be removed and which tied down to provide an effective framework. It is satisfying to see the job when it is finished, and it is even more rewarding to see the results a few months later when it produces masses of flowers. The more one learns about pruning, the more enjoyable the task becomes.

I think it is fair to say that hardly a day goes by in the garden when I am not prompted to smile by something I see. I am often asked if I ever find time to sit. The answer is not very often because I prefer to wander slowly round on my own so that I don't miss things, and it is usually on these strolls that I find myself smiling.

Finally, it is hard not to respond with a smile to the hugely generous and complimentary comments made by visitors. Nothing could be more rewarding for a gardener.

Gardening Techniques

It is difficult to know where to begin on this huge subject, and I am only going to attempt to describe some of the more basic methods and practices we use as we garden.

TOOLS

During the summer months we use border forks for weeding and forking over where we have trodden on the soil, but during the winter months when we are more likely to be digging up heavier clumps of plants and dividing them, we also use larger forks with longer tines and heavier duty spades. When we set off with our barrows, apart from being equipped with our own secateurs, we take a lot of plastic buckets with handles used for collecting weeds, top growth to compost, plants dug up for the nursery, and sinking pots into water before planting, but we also take a large pot containing a pocket saw, trowels, hand forks, Japanese hori hori knives (which are particularly useful for extracting tap-rooted weeds), black plastic labels and a silver pen, and a ball of flexible tie. When we need them we take loppers as well.

PLANTING

Usually we will be adding several plants to form a group, in which case having cleaned the area of weeds we will dig it over with a big fork and, if necessary, add some of our own compost to improve the soil. Meanwhile the plants will be held down in a bucket of water until no more bubbles emerge, indicating that the compost has completely absorbed the water. They are positioned (in their pots) spaced out in advance of planting. A hole is then dug with a spade bigger than the pot size so that the roots will be able to penetrate the surrounding soil. Unless the soil is already damp from rain, we will also pour water into the hole. When the plant is taken out of the pot it may be rootbound; if so, we use the blunt part of the secateurs to tease the roots apart or, if they are very tightly bound, cut through them to break them up. We then sprinkle some bonemeal in the hole, which should encourage root growth, before placing the plant in the hole, the soil replaced and firmed down. This exercise will then be repeated for the rest. And, most importantly, a label is placed at the front of the group. If we are planting in spring or summer, we will probably sprinkle blood, fish and bone under plants instead of bonemeal as that encourages foliage and flower as well as root growth.

FEEDING AND COMPOSTING

Apart from using bonemeal through the winter months and blood, fish and bone during the spring and summer when planting, we hardly do any feeding. The nursery plants are grown in a peat-free compost with added grit and slow-release Osmocote, so all the tender plants which we plant out in terracotta and other pots for the summer do not need additional feeding during their season outside. We do, however, give repeat-flowering roses a handful of chicken pellets just as the first flush of flowers is starting to fade, and all the roses are given a good mulch of manure in spring. In the autumn we have a huge leaf fall which is cleared and piled up to create leaf mould. This is normally ready to use by the following autumn. We also have several compost heaps round the garden which are fed with spent growth from plants, lawn mowings and used compost. This will be turned over in the autumn and should be fit to use by the following spring. As we garden on clay soil, we often need to improve the ground before doing a new planting, and this is when (after digging over the ground) we will add both leaf mould and our own compost to lighten the soil. If it is particularly heavy, we may also add some of the burnt soil from under the bonfire and possibly some gravel to help improve the drainage.

DIVISION

During the winter we quite often decide to dig up a whole group of one plant, sometimes because we want to move it, but more likely because it is tired and in need of division. It gives us an opportunity to discard the old centres of the plants, to split up the newer parts and improve the soil before replanting some of the divisions – the rest go to the nursery for propagation. Usually the division is done by putting two equal-sized forks back to back against each other through the plant into the ground, then pushing them together before pulling them apart and hopefully dividing the plant at that point. With some plants with more solid root structures like hemerocallis and hostas, it is generally easier to divide them with a sharp spade.

CUTTING BACK

I think one of the hardest things for gardeners to do is to bring themselves to cut back plants before the last flower has died. Over the years I have disciplined myself to be ruthless in this respect. It begins with hellebores where we cut all the old leaves off just after Christmas. This allows the emerging flowers to be seen and avoids flowers being cut by mistake along with old leaves if it is left too late. It also exposes the plant, removing cover for mice who like to nibble the buds, which can certainly be a problem in our garden. The next group of plants to be cut back for the same reason is epimediums, which we generally do around the end of January, thus enabling their delicate flowers to be visible when they come through rather than being swamped by old foliage. After this, there is an interval before it is necessary to cut back the spent flowers and foliage of plants such as pulmonarias, brunneras and early hardy geraniums once they have finished their main flowering. This will result in new foliage growth and in some cases a second flush of flowers, and in any event they will look better than leaving old foliage, which can often become mildewed. In late March and early April depending on the season, we will cut back the foliage of libertias and dieramas. Both these plants are evergreen, and if not cut back at this stage the old leaves start to go brown alongside the new ones, which is not a good look when the plant is flowering. The winter-flowering iris, *I. stylosa*, can present the same problem. It may continue flowering into the spring, but I try and remember to cut the leaves back in early summer to encourage new leaf growth. During the summer months we continue to cut back foliage and flowers on plants such as geum, nepeta, later flowering geraniums, delphinium, early aconitums, centaurea, diascia, *Viola cornuta*, dianthus, galega, echinops, eryngium, etc. The list is endless, but it really does make a difference and most of them will flower again. We always marvel how much better a border looks when groups of plants have been cut back here and there, especially in late summer. In larger borders it seems to add a different dimension when plants are no longer all the same height; you can suddenly see through to others that were previously not visible, and in a curious way it gives the border a greater sense of depth.

DEADHEADING

This is a form of summer manicuring, but it can also be a therapeutic pastime and can transform a plant. The ones which we find ourselves doing regularly are centaureas, geums, roses, dahlias, heleniums, echinaceas, knautias, some asters and clematis. *Helenium* 'Sahin's Early Flowerer' looks like a completely different plant after it has been deadheaded, although I have to admit it takes a long time to do.

PRUNING

As a general rule the best time to prune a shrub is after flowering has finished. It is easier said than done because there comes a stage in summer when so many are in flower. But not all shrubs need to be pruned every year: probably at least every three years or so will suffice to encourage new growth from the bottom of the plant. In theory this is achieved by taking roughly one-third of the oldest stems from the base of the plant. Evergreen shrubs which flower late in the season such as abelia, myrtle (*Myrtus communis*) and some forms of escallonia are best left until the spring to prune in case their new growth is damaged by winter frosts. Evergreen topiary shrubs like box, holly, phillyrea and yew tend to be clipped rather than pruned and in the case of box is best done in spring when it is neither sunny nor frosty. We tend to prune roses as and when we get to them in the borders from November onwards. After removing dead and diseased wood, we prune shrub roses hard. With climbing roses we try to spread the main branches as horizontally as possible to maximize the flowering potential of dormant buds, although depending on the space available this is not always easy to achieve. On the whole, we leave rambling roses to their own devices unless they are interfering with other plants or have dangling branches. As I have mentioned in the chapter on clematis above, we have mainly Group 3 clematis in the garden, which need pruning to a few inches above ground in late winter or early spring. The earlier flowering clematis just need tidying up, and montanas only need to be taken right down

occasionally when they have become too big, to encourage new growth from the base.

PROTECTING CLEMATIS AGAINST MICE

Mice love to chew the new shoots of clematis, so we use round black plastic pots with the bottom cut out and place the pot upside down over the clematis, pushing it hard into the soil to anchor it. This seems to discourage the mice and also protects the new shoots from the sun.

PLANT SUPPORTS

We use hazel to make supports for plants. This is a job best done in April when hazel is still green enough to bend and before plants get too big. With free-standing clematis we make a wigwam shape, while for herbaceous plants such as delphiniums, tall asters and some aconitums, we make a more rounded framework for them to grow through. For dahlias we use circular metal grids on legs as they need firmer support.

CHELSEA CHOP

The idea is to reduce the growth on some perennial plants towards the end of May, which will delay flowering but produce stronger plants with better flowers. We do this with *Campanula lactiflora*, border phlox and some asters, and it seems to work. I know some people adopt this practice with sedums (renamed hylotelephium) to stop them from splitting late in summer. However, we prefer to lift those vulnerable upright sedums, such as *S.* 'Autumn Joy', *Sedum* (syn. *Hylotelephium*) 'Matrona', *S. spectabile* and *S. telephium* 'Xenox', in winter when going through the borders. If the plant is too large, we will divide it at this stage and give divisions to the nursery. Otherwise, we just redig the hole and place it back with no food but water if necessary and firm it down. This seems to check the tendency to split in late summer. But it is not necessary to do this with the lower growing varieties.

DOUBLE PLANTING

It is sometimes worth thinking about using a space for two different types of plant. There are a number of early spring plants, mainly bulbs, which are summer dormant, and it makes sense to use a space twice rather than leave the ground looking vacant for a period of the year.

In the top and drier part of the Bog Garden I have planted the bright yellow *Erythronium tuolumnense* among *Filipendula rubra* and *Persicaria polymorpha*. This provides a carpet of bright yellow in March when neither the filipendula nor the persicaria is showing signs of life and coincides with the similar colour of *Lysichiton americanus*, *Fritillaria imperialis* and forsythia in the Water Garden above. We have an early narcissus growing through a planting of *Hosta* 'Thomas Hogg' in the Water Garden, snowdrops under hydrangeas, blue chionodoxa through the maidenhair fern (*Adiantum venustum*), *Anemone nemorosa* and white chionodoxa through groups of autumn cyclamen. In a different way, when we lift tulips after flowering, we use the spaces for dahlias, annuals and tender perennials.

COLLECTING SEEDS

Apart from providing the nursery with plant material for division, as gardeners we are obviously best placed to collect seeds when they are ripe. So in the later part of summer we add old envelopes and pencils to our pot of small tools, and when we spot a plant which has gone to seed we shake them into an envelope, label the envelope, and give them to the nursery to be dried and cleaned up and transferred to small envelopes until the time is right for them to be sown.

ROSE REPLANT DISEASE

There is a risk that this will occur when planting a rose where one has been before. And if it does the new rose tends not to flourish. To counteract this risk, as we had to do when we replanted the Rose Walk fairly recently, we put the roses in reasonably deep cardboard boxes, filling up the boxes with a mixture of clean soil, manure and the compost from the pot. The theory is that by the time the cardboard has rotted sufficiently for the rose roots to make contact with the soil, it should no longer be contaminated. This process probably slows down the initial growth of the rose, but it seems to combat the problem of rose replant disease. I believe that mycorrhizal fungi (which can be bought in powdered form and sprinkled into the soil when planting) can also be used to protect the roots from this disease, but I haven't tried it here.

MAKING NOTES

During August and September we start making notes about what we might like to change, move or add to the garden. Gardens don't stand still and need constant 'editing'. Plants die or get too big or we tire of them; places have to be found for new plants; a colour scheme needs to be improved or something has to be resited in a better position. It is amazing how easy it is to talk about a potential improvement and to have completely forgotten about it a few months later. So it is really worth writing ideas down as they are discussed.

PUTTING THE GARDEN TO BED

This is the title of a lecture which I have given on several occasions when we were running our Garden School courses here. I am frequently asked by visitors how we manage the garden in winter, and as that is the time when we undertake most of our serious and challenging garden work, the following is a brief description of the sort of jobs we do. While we are still open in September we usually tidy up and weed the Woodland Garden, because this is the first area to perform in late winter and early spring.

As I have mentioned above, after making notes about changes we wish to implement, we embark on the more significant ones once the garden is closed in October. This usually involves work in the borders where we are planning more than just digging up one group of plants to improve the soil and replant them. It is so much easier to make substantial changes when we can still see the shapes, heights and colours of surrounding plants rather than struggling to remember those details in mid-winter when everything has died down and looks the same.

From the beginning of November we start planting tulips, and always commence with the Acacia Border because this is the first one to come to life in the spring. We cut back and lift dahlias after removing their frames, and hand them to the nursery staff to be thoroughly dried out, after which they are stored in boxes underneath the potting shed benches. In the spring they will be divided for propagation, potted up, and put outside with protective covering until it is warm enough to leave them exposed. We lift dahlias partly to create space for tulips and partly because it gives an opportunity to divide and propagate from the larger clumps.

We then embark on cutting back the top growth on all herbaceous plants except for those like penstemons, hardy salvias and lobelias, which may be reduced by half to avoid windrock but will not be cut right back until they start to shoot in the spring. Leaving some top growth on these slightly less hardy perennials provides a bit of protection against severe winter weather. Annuals are removed and the ground is weeded, forked over and improved with compost and leaf mould if necessary. At this stage we will prune roses and carry out further planting changes indicated in our notes. We put bamboo sticks in potential tulip positions to ensure they are well spread out, making use of vacated dahlia spots, and then proceed to plant the tulips. We normally put 20 or 25 in a hole according to the space and tulips available and, depending on the size of the border, will probably plant approximately ten groups. Where we have had a problem with tulip fire, often caused by repeated planting, we layer tulips in deep pots filled with potting compost and place the pots just below the surface of the soil so their roots will not contact the soil. This works for the most part, although the bulbs are more vulnerable to interference by squirrels and we often have to protect them with chicken wire. We attempt to repeat this procedure throughout the beds in the top part of the garden, the Water Garden and the Mediterranean Bank before Christmas, leaving the lower part until after the New Year. With so many beds and borders there are plenty of areas for wildlife to overwinter in the dead and decaying foliage yet to be cleared.

In early spring we start to cut back shrubs which will flower on the current year's growth such as santolina and other silver- and grey-leaf shrubs, buddleja, the paniculata and arborescens forms of hydrangea, deciduous ceanothus, caryopteris and many others. This will also apply to penstemons, lobelias and shrubby salvias; in all these cases the rule is to wait until the shrub or plant is showing signs of new growth, when it is deemed to be safe to cut it back.

I should emphasise that as a garden which opens in mid-February for snowdrops and hellebores, this is the routine we have adopted so that it looks presentable for visitors at that point. However, for gardens whose owners are not concerned about opening for visitors, apart from planting tulips, much of the above work could be carried out in March and April.

Plants: Friends and Foes

During the thirty plus years that I have been gardening at Coton, I have built up a considerable amount of knowledge about the behaviour of our plants, and this chapter is designed to inform readers about the merits and defects of some of them. I would like to stress that this is a somewhat subjective exercise because we garden in the Midlands on clay, and plants may behave differently in other climatic and soil conditions. Also, some people may be happier with plants that I would regard as invasive because they do not have the time or inclination to control them. After all, it would be very boring if all gardeners had the same preferences – part of the fun of visiting other gardens is to see plants we do not know and others we have rejected being used successfully in a different context. So what follows is just a summation of various plants we have in the garden, some which make a fleeting appearance, others which give a reliable performance, some with shortcomings and others with health warnings. The list of plants I have tried and rejected over the years is too long to recite here, and I am only reminded of them when searching through plant nursery lists.

SHOWSTOPPERS

This category includes those plants which we can't resist because they provide a fleeting visual feast for the eyes and most of them do not flower for long. The luxury of a garden this size is that we can accommodate quite a number of these prima donnas, but we have to choose their locations with care.

Perennials

Delphinium – we only have a few, 'Finsteraarhorn' and 'Faust' being my favourites. They require strong supports, but I wouldn't like to be without them for their colour and stature in the borders and, if we are lucky, their second flowering.

Dictamnus albus var. *purpureus* – erect stems with lily-shaped, pale mauve flowers veined with purple in early summer and strongly aromatic leaves, quite difficult to establish but well worth the effort.

Erythronium – in particular, *E. californicum* 'White Beauty' and *E.* 'Pagoda' are delightful in the Woodland Garden in March/April.

Iris, bearded – all are beautiful, but while their foliage is elegant in early summer it can prove problematic later on.

Iris sibirica 'Silver Edge' – in my opinion this is the most eye-catching of all Siberian irises.

Meconopsis betonicifolia – this is one of nature's most exquisite plants, and we can just keep them going in our garden, given our pH of 6.5.

Papaver orientale (oriental poppy) – ethereal but fleeting, and post-flowering foliage needs to be cut back and disguised.

Peony, herbaceous – 'Sarah Bernhardt' and 'Duchesse de Nemours' are both stunning.

Peony, Itoh hybrids or intersectional – our favourites are 'Cora Louise', 'Copper Kettle', 'Hillary' and 'Sonoma Blessing'.

Peony, species – I favour *Paeonia tenuifolia* and *P. veitchii* in this group.

Phlox divaricata subsp. *laphamii* 'Chattahoochee' – a showstopper which flowers longer than most of the others mentioned above.

Roscoea cautleyoides – a delicate, pale yellow, orchid-like flower in July and August.

Shrubs

Cornus 'Eddie's White Wonder' – provides a glorious show in late May/early June.

Deutzia setchuenensis var. *corymbiflora* – as the name implies, charming corymbs of white flowers in June.

Magnolia grandiflora 'Exmouth' – huge creamy white flowers at intervals in late summer, strongly scented.

Paeonia rockii hybrid – the ultimate ephemeral but irresistible flowering shrub.

Rhododendron luteum – beautiful yellow flowers with evocative scent.

Syringa meyeri 'Palibin' – lower growing form of lilac with the most intense scent in May.

STALWARTS

These are plants which give the best value through the summer in terms of length of flowering and good foliage. The list would be too long if I were to mention all the cultivars under each heading, so I have just included what I regard as the best examples.

Perennials

Agapanthus – my favoured ones are 'Blue Moon', 'Navy Blue' and 'Sandringham'.

Artemisia alba 'Canascens' – a lovely filigree silver-leaf plant (technically a subshrub).

Aster × frikartii 'Mönch' – an outstanding mid-blue aster which flowers from July to November.

Astrantia major – our preferences are 'Gill Richardson' and 'Shaggy'.

Brunnera – 'Jack Frost' and 'Looking Glass' with their silvered foliage light up and can cope in dry shade and are not invasive like the species *B. macrophylla*.

Campanula lactiflora – the sort of self-seeder we welcome in many parts of the garden with its lovely blue flowers.

Clematis, climbing – 'Black Prince' (dark purple), 'Princess Diana' (strong pink) and 'Lord Lambton' (strong yellow with lovely seed heads) all provide long flowering periods.

Clematis, herbaceous – *C. heracleifolia* 'Cassandra' is long flowering with scented deep blue flowers.

Clematis, semi-herbaceous – 'Arabella', *C. integrifolia* and 'Petit Faucon', in shades of blue and purple, all give a long flowering performance if regularly deadheaded.

Dahlia – favourites include 'Allan Sparkes', 'Café au Lait', 'Labyrinth', 'Le Baron' and 'Thomas A. Edison'.

Geranium – 'Anne Thomson', 'Ann Folkard', 'Rozanne, *G. sanguineum* 'Elke' and *G. sanguineum* var. *striatum* are the most reliable long-flowering hardy geraniums which only need minimal tidying up (as opposed to cutting back hard) and are all pleasing, useful colours.

Helenium 'Sahin's Early Flowerer' – a brilliant long-performing plant for the hot border.

Heuchera – 'Chocolate Ruffles', 'Obsidian' and 'Palace Purple' are all good foils for other plants.

Hosta – *H. fortunei*, 'Halcyon', 'Honeybells' and *H. sieboldiana* 'Elegans' all appeal to me and less so to slugs and snails.

Penstemon – 'Apple Blossom', 'Countess of Dalkeith', 'Hidcote Pink' and 'King George V' are the most reliable in our garden.

Sedum (syn. *Hylotelephium*) – one of the most useful plants for a border, looking good from the time its fleshy leaves emerge in spring to the end of summer when it flowers. Favourites are 'Bertram Anderson', 'Matrona', *S. spectabile*, *S. telephium* 'Xenox' and 'Vera Jameson'.

Shrubs

Choisya ternata – excellent for dry shade where its white flowers and light reflective leaves shine out and it produces a reliable second flowering in late summer.

Daphne bholua 'Jacqueline Postill' – a remarkably beautiful and relatively easy daphne whose scented pink flowers last from January into March.

Euphorbia – *E. characias* hybrids, *E. myrsinites* and *E. wallichii* are all invaluable contributors to the garden.

Hydrangea – *H. arborescens* 'Annabelle', *H. paniculata* 'Limelight', *H. serrata* 'Preziosa' and *H. serrata* 'Uzu-azisai' all flower for a long time with beautiful blooms.

Philadelphus 'Belle Etoile' – outstanding amongst other philadelphus, especially for its scent.

Rose, shrub – impossible to name all my favourites, but these are a few I would never want to be without: 'Ghislaine de Féligonde', 'Lady Emma Hamilton', 'Little White Pet' and 'Mutabilis'.

Rose, climbing – 'Cooper's Burmese' is a lovely climber with white flowers and excellent dark green foliage which attracts more comments than any other of the many roses in the garden. *R. multiflora* 'Platyphylla' (Seven Sisters' rose) adorns the front of the house, and 'Autumn Sunset' is a glorious warm yellow.

Salvia – 'Amistad', 'Javier', 'Lalarsha', 'Nachtvlinder', 'Penny's Smile' and 'Sungold' have all proved their worth in terms of colour, reliability and flowering time.

UNDERVALUED PLANTS

These plants are understated by comparison with those above, and some of them less well known, but nonetheless make an important contribution to the garden and mostly perform for a long period.

Perennials

Agastache 'Black Adder' and 'Blue Fortune' – valuable, long-flowering blue forms of anise hyssop which provide a strong vertical emphasis in any border.

Althaea armeniaca – lovely tall, wandy stems with masses of small pale pink flowers, useful for late summer in the border.

Anaphalis triplinervis 'Summer Snow' – white flowers with silver/grey foliage, useful in sunny conditions and, unusually for grey-leaf plants, performs in dryish shade.

Aster divaricatus (syn. *Eurybia divaricata*) – a really invaluable plant with masses of small white daisy flowers from midsummer onwards, with dark green foliage and dark red stems, which does particularly well in dry shade.

Campanula – 'Crystal' has pale blue bells which if deadheaded last for the main part of summer, and an unnamed campanula (traditionally known to us as *Campanula symphyandra*) is a low-growing and more ground-covering form with similar flowers.

Cyclamen hederifolium – enchanting white and pink flowers from August onwards, followed by marbled leaves which last through winter and into spring.

Epimedium – one of the most undervalued groups of woodland plants, with very delicate flowers in spring followed by pretty foliage lasting through the rest of the year. My favourite and most reliable one is *E. × versicolor* 'Sulphureum', which has very pale yellow flowers.

Eupatorium rugosum – flowers in later summer for a long time with loose round heads of white flowers, and it doesn't mind growing in dry shade. I hope readers will understand my obsession with dry shade, but we have a considerable amount of it in this garden and it isn't always easy to find plants that will flourish in these conditions, so I really value those that do.

Ferns – one of the true pleasures in spring is to observe ferns uncoiling as they start into growth, and once they are in full leaf they are all in their different quiet ways exquisitely beautiful. I believe they are underappreciated partly because in botanical Latin they all start with different names, which is very confusing, so I am only going to mention two types: polystichum ferns, which flourish in dry shade, of which my favourite is *Polystichum setiferum* 'Pulcherrimum Bevis', and *Asplenium scolopendrium*, the heart's tongue fern, with lovely shiny, tongue-shaped, reflective leaves lighting up shady areas. There are so many more to enjoy – it is worth exploring them all.

Galtonia candicans – large white bells on tall stems, a bulbous perennial which makes a graceful addition to the border in midsummer.

Gillenia trifoliata – masses of small delicate white flowers on dark red stems flourishing in partial shade, with dark green leaves which turn a shade of rusty orange in autumn.

Iris pallida 'Argentea Variegata' – this plant is primarily grown for its beautiful variegated foliage, which unlike most irises remains looking good for most of the summer months, but it also has pretty blue flowers.

Oxalis articulata – this is a pretty small plant with deep pink flowers and glaucous foliage, unlike its more pernicious relative which we spend a lot of time trying to eradicate.

Pachysandra terminalis – an attractive ground-cover plant, also good in its variegated form, which favours dry shade.

Primula elatior – the oxlip is the lesser known cousin of the primrose and cowslip, and in some ways I think it has a more enchanting habit with a head of delicate yellow flowers on a single stem.

Persicaria amplexicaulis 'Alba' – its slender white flower spires can cope with dry shade and look particularly effective against a dark green background.

Tricyrtis stolonifera – the toad lily has mauve flowers speckled with dark purple spots quite late in the season that remain for a good length of time.

Shrubs

Caryopteris × clandonensis 'Heavenly Blue' – an excellent late flowering shrub with beautiful blue flowers and greyish foliage.

Ceratostigma willmottianum – long flowering during the second part of summer, enjoys the protection of a warm wall and produces truly royal blue flowers.

Cornus kousa – a lovely shrub which in our garden produces variable amounts of creamy white bracts with small flowers in June.

Cornus mas – an elegant spreading shrub with yellow flowers in March and dark red fruit in the autumn.

Fuchsia magellanica 'Alba' – unlike its showier cousins, it is totally hardy and has the most delicate pale pink (not white, despite the name) flowers.

Ribes sanguineum 'White Icicle' – stunningly beautiful with racemes of white flowers in early spring and one of my favourites.

Sarcococca ruscifolia – evergreen with highly scented white flowers in winter.

PLANTS WITH GOOD FOLIAGE AFTER FLOWERING

While many earlier flowering plants respond well to being cut back hard once flowering has finished, resulting in fresh new foliage and sometimes a second flowering, it is always hard to find plants where the foliage remains looking good after flowering without needing to be cut down. These are ones I would recommend.

Amsonia – *A. tabernaemontana* and *A. orientalis* (formerly *Rhazya orientalis*) both keep their foliage, which in the case of the former turns to gold in the autumn, less so with the latter. *A. tabernaemontana* is taller and has pale blue flowers in June, while *A. orientalis* is shorter and has deeper blue flowers which last a lot longer.

Baptisia australis – this plant has lovely blue, lupin-like flowers in early summer, and its excellent, slightly glaucous foliage continues to look attractive for the rest of summer.

Convallaria majalis – lily of the valley leaves remain good after its beautiful flowers have finished.

Disporum cantoniense 'Green Giant' – a beautiful tall woodland plant with branching evergreen foliage and creamy green bells.

Helleborus × hybridus – there are many forms of this lovely early spring-flowering plant, where the new leaves follow the flowers and if kept disease-free remain looking good for the rest of the year.

Lathyrus vernus – the spring-flowering pea is ideal for woodland planting and retains its good foliage throughout summer.

Polygonatum × hybridum – commonly known as Solomon's seal, with branches of white bells in spring, it continues to have good foliage for the rest of summer provided it is kept free of sawfly, which can reduce its leaves to lace (we spray once with insecticide when it has leafed up).

Thermopsis lanceolata – has yellow lupin-like flowers in late spring, while the leaves maintain their freshness for a large part of the summer.

FAVOURITE ANNUALS

Acidanthera bicolor (also known as *Gladiolus* 'Murieliae') – elegant white flowers with dark maroon centres, sold by bulb suppliers, good for late summer (a perennial that we treat as an annual as it is not hardy and does not flower after being overwintered in a pot).

Agrostemma 'Ocean Pearl' – a beautiful white form of corncockle.

Antirrhinum 'Black Prince' – a very dark red form of snapdragon.

Cleome hassleriana – we use purple, pink and white forms of this spider plant.

Hibiscus trionum – stunning cream flowers with dark maroon centres, which we are constantly being asked to identify.

Nicotiana – we use *N. langsdorffii*, 'Lime Green', *N. mutabilis*, *N. sylvestris*, *N. suaveolens* and 'Tinkerbell'.

Nigella damascena 'Miss Jekyll – this love-in-a-mist has pretty blue flowers and charming seed heads.

Orlaya grandiflora – lacy white flowers in early summer, very pretty, but needs to be replaced by July.

Tagetes 'Cinnabar' – a really good form of dark red marigold.

PLANTS THAT NEED SCREENING AFTER FLOWERING

Aconitum – early to mid-season flowering forms such as *A. anglicum*, 'Bressingham Spire' and 'Spark's Variety' do not produce either new flowers or fresh leaves after being cut back and will need to be planted behind a later flowering perennial or a shrub that has been cut back in the spring.

Delphinium – needs to be cut back after the first flowering and will leaf up again and sometimes, depending on the weather and where it is planted, flower again. However, it does need to be screened after being cut back.

Hardy geranium – most geraniums benefit from being cut back, particularly the earlier flowering ones, which otherwise tend to develop mildewed and unattractive foliage. So it's probably best not to place them in frontal positions in a border. The earlier they are cut back, the quicker they leaf up and flower again.

Hemerocallis – I think this definitely needs to be cut back following flowering because the leaves tend to become a mess, so it then needs to be disguised with other planting. In our garden there is one exception, the early flowering 'Golden Chimes', which, cut back promptly after flowering, recovers and will flower again.

Lupin – there comes a point when it is no longer worth deadheading lupins and they need to be cut down. They never really recover and are best screened.

Papaver orientale – another plant that does not perform again after its first flowering and should be well disguised thereafter.

PLANTS WITH A HEALTH WARNING

Acanthus spinosus – a handsome plant but almost impossible to eradicate.

Anchusa officinalis – I am still trying to eliminate this after three decades.

Anemone, summer flowering – one of my favourite plants but difficult to move or remove, particularly *A. tomentosa* 'Robustissima'.

Arum italicum var. *pictum* – attractive variegated leaves for dry woodland but incredibly invasive and impossible to eradicate.

Brunnera macrophylla – lovely blue flowers but has a huge tendency to seed itself beyond its remit.

Bidens heterophylla – a tall plant with delicate, very pale yellow flowers and an excellent foil for the stronger colours of late summer, but we have to surround it with a corset of slate at ground level to try and impede its tendency to take over the border. In its defence it flowers into late autumn and makes excellent cut flowers with a delectable scent if picked for the house.

Clerodendrum bungei – only by being isolated on an island on the pond, where it is shown to great advantage, have we managed to contain its suckering habit.

Eryngium – plants I would not want to be without, but, as with anemones, challenging to dig up without leaving some behind that will regrow.

Geranium nodosum – in our garden this pretty pink-flowered woodlander is the ultimate seeder and we have developed our own verb: to 'de-nodosum'. The seedlings need to be dug out with a fork.

Lamium – this plant has an invasive habit and we only grow its more refined *L. maculata* forms.

Miscanthus – difficult to manage because plants increase in size very quickly and in my experience need at least two people to dig up to split down to a plantable size again.

Ornithogalum umbellatum – star of Bethlehem is a pretty but invasive spring-flowering bulb.

Symphytum – all forms of comfrey are good ground cover for shady areas but need to be contained, especially the white-flowered form, which seeds itself everywhere if given the opportunity.

Thalictrum flavum subsp. *glaucum* – pretty, tall, fluffy yellow flower heads but has a strong tendency to seed itself.

Frequently Asked Questions

These often comprise questions for which there is no single or specific answer – the most classic one being:

What is your favourite flower?

This is truly impossible to answer. It will probably depend on when it is asked and what has been or is in flower at that moment which has caused me to stop and marvel. Flowering plants and shrubs have such varying qualities of ephemerality, long performance, distinctive foliage and scent that it is impossible to single out one in favour of others. However, if I am pushed into giving an answer, I would probably suggest roses as my favourites. Within this genus there are so many cultivars, colours, shapes, scents and habits which between them last over a very long period of time that it is hard to think of any other group of plants which together give me so much delight and pleasure.

How do you protect your hostas from slugs and snails?

We don't do anything to them, which is probably the most infuriating answer the questioner wants to hear. I then go on to suggest that to some extent the presence of so many birds in the garden probably reduces the population of these pests; because we have so many groups of hostas in the garden and can only thin them out infrequently, to some extent the thickness of the clumps can disguise signs of chewing, but we don't use any pesticide control on them.

Which is your favourite part of the garden?

I think that people are often surprised by my answer, which is the Woodland Garden. Because there are so many colourfully planted areas, they might expect me to name one of those, but it is the woodland area that I enjoy most. In a way it is strange because it is the nearest part of the garden to the road and therefore the sound of traffic, but for me it has a very special atmosphere which is hard to define. I think it is a combination of the glade of mature woodland trees, the view from the gate running down to the 36-ha/90-acre reservoir below the garden rising up the other side of the valley, and perhaps most important of all the gentle and understated type of plants which enjoy growing under deciduous trees. I find that all this contributes to a sense of peace.

How much help do you have in the garden?

A difficult question to answer because aside from myself and Richard Green, who work full time, I have several part-time helpers who do a morning, a day or two days a week and not always in school holidays and half-terms. But in terms of hours worked, and including myself, it is probably the equivalent of more than three full-time people and less than four.

What is your favourite season?

Another question that prompts a surprise answer, which is winter. So much of what we do in the garden is with the future in mind, and during the winter months when the garden is closed we are able to carry out changes, or 'editing' as I like to describe it. This then prompts me to look forward to the effect that these changes will bring several months later in the next season. Each season has its special delights, but there is something about the austerity of winter – the exquisite silhouettes of trees, especially when seen against a blue sky; the strong scents of winter-flowering shrubs; the ephemeral and heart-stopping sunsets which no painting can ever quite capture; the constant companionship of robins and the joy of hearing their songs; and the anticipation of everything to come with buds appearing on trees and shrubs – that I find exhilarating. It is a season that clears the palate and allows one to slow down and really appreciate every winter flower as it appears, before there is so much happening in a garden the size of ours that it is difficult to take it all in.

Do you lift your tulips after flowering?

The answer is 'yes', except for a few species tulips, all of which are reliably perennial, such as *Tulipa saxatilis* on the Mediterranean Bank, *T. sylvestris* in the orchards and *T. sprengeri* in the Rose Walk. The hybrid tulips we plant thousands of every year do not generally produce a reliable second flowering. Their bulbs divide underground, so they take time to build up to flowering strength, and (depending on the variety and the soil conditions in which they are grown) can be subject to insect damage and rotting. There are undoubtedly certain tulips which are more reliable than others, and in our experience 'Spring Green' (Viridiflora Group), which we plant singly in the orchards after they have flowered, is best at reflowering after a year or two. A further reason is that we need the space the tulips occupied for dahlias and tender plants which will be planted out from the end of May.

When do you cut back hellebore leaves?

The answer is from late December into January. The reason is partly to remove the risk of passing on disease from the old foliage to the new, as hellebores are susceptible to a form of black spot, and by this stage they are probably starting to fade and droop. But it is also so that the new flowers, which appear before the new foliage, can be seen and enjoyed.

Do you leave dahlias in the ground?

We do leave species dahlias in the ground, in our case *D. sherffii* and *D. merckii*, because they seem to cope better with winter conditions in the garden. However, we lift all the cultivars, partly because on balance they survive better if, after being cut down, they are thoroughly dried out and then stored in a dry place in the potting shed over winter. This frees up space in the garden that we need for tulip planting, and also it allows us to divide bigger dahlia tubers in the spring for propagation purposes before being potted up in late March or early April.

How old are your flamingos?

We think that the two deeper coloured Caribbean flamingos and the slightly smaller pale one which we believe to be of Chilean origin arrived at Coton around 1970, although we have no idea how old they were then! The four taller pale African flamingos joined the older three in 2018. They are much younger, but we don't have their date of birth.

When do you cut your Wildflower Meadow?

The meadow is usually cut towards the end of July, although it will depend to some extent on how the knapweed is performing. Sometimes we need to cut it earlier to avoid it seeding, because it can easily become too dominant if allowed to seed freely. And on a more practical note, it is somewhat dependent on when we can persuade the farmer to cut, turn and bale the hay for us, as it is always a very busy time of year for farmers.

How do you garden with bantams running free?

This is undoubtedly a challenge. It is not too much of a problem when the ground becomes covered in foliage, but while there are still bare patches of soil where we have been digging, the bantams busy themselves looking for worms and sometimes eating young foliage. After that time they are really not a bother, and they do entertain us with their antics.

Identifying plants

This is obviously the most frequent question, although it is much easier now that visitors are able to show us on their phones what they wish to have identified. And even that involves fewer questions these days because of the phone apps which claim to identify plants. Personally, I don't find these apps to be very accurate and I think it is better to ask if there is someone available to help. We also label plants, but as the season progresses labels can become camouflaged under foliage so are not always visible.

What sort of soil does your garden have?

We garden on clay with a pH of approximately 6.5 (slightly acid). Most areas have been improved over the years with a combination of cow manure, our own garden compost and leaf mould, but we are always finding more parts that need improving so it is an ongoing process. Clay soil is good because it holds nutrients and roses enjoy it, but it is not easy in very dry conditions, when cracks can develop, or in wet conditions when it becomes heavy and unworkable.

What do you do with your pelargoniums in winter?

All the plants in pots, including pelargoniums, that we display outside in summer need winter protection. After closing the garden at the end of September, the pots are assembled in the Stable Yard, where final cuttings can be taken and they can be covered with fleece if there is an early frost. Most will be cut back roughly by half in order to reduce their bulk and enable us to fit them into our polytunnel for the winter, which we keep frost-free with a thermostat that should prevent the temperature dropping below 6°C/43°F. During this period they are watered only occasionally and lightly. From January onwards, on days when we are unable to work in the garden due to extreme weather, we start to empty the pots, prune the tops and roots of plants quite hard, and repot them in fresh compost containing slow-release fertilizer. Where necessary they will be replaced with new plants.

Plants in Major Borders

SOUTH-WEST TERRACE

Agapanthus africanus (wooden boxes)
Agapanthus 'Doctor Brouwer'
Alchemilla mollis
Allium cristophii
Artemisia canescens
Artemisia nutans
Artemisia schmidtiana 'Nana' (sink)
Artemisia splendens
Campanula poscharskyana
Centranthus ruber
Chionodoxa 'Pink Giant'
Cistus 'Grayswood Pink'
Clematis rehderiana
Clematis viticella 'Madame Julia Correvon'
Clematis viticella 'Odoriba'
Convolvulus cneorum (sink)
Dahlia 'Purple Gem'
Dianthus 'Pink Jewel' (sink)
Erigeron karvinskianus
Erodium chrysanthemum (sink)
Erysimum 'Bowles's Mauve'
Galanthus nivalis
Galanthus 'Strathan'
Geranium sanguineum 'Elke'
Geranium sanguineum var. *striatum*
Helleborus 'Magic Leaves'
Helleborus 'Winter Star'
Heuchera 'Obsidian'
Iris stylosa
Leucojum autumnale (sink)
Libertia grandiflora (syn. *L. chilensis*)

Osmanthus delavayi
Penstemon 'Countess of Dalkeith'
Penstemon 'Raven'
Phlox divaricata subsp. *laphamii* 'Chattahoochee' (sink)
Rosa banksiae 'Lutea'
Rosa 'Mermaid'
Rosa multiflora 'Platyphylla' (Seven Sisters' rose)
Salvia 'Lalarsha'
Salvia microphylla 'Pink Blush'
Salvia 'Nachtvlinder'
Sedum 'Schorbuser Blut' (sink)
Sedum spurium (sink)
Sempervivum 'Walcott's Variety' (sink)
Senecio viravira
Syringa meyeri 'Palibin'
Thymus serpyllum (sink)
Thymus vulgaris 'Silver Posie' (sink)
Trachelospermum asiaticum
Tulipa 'Gorilla'
Tulipa 'Spring Green'

ACACIA BORDER

Allium 'Purple Sensation'
Althea armenica
Anemone hupehensis 'Prinz Heinrich'
Anemone × *hybrida* 'Honorine Jobert'
Anemone × *hybrida* 'Robustissima'
Anemone × *hybrida* 'September Charm'
Aquilegia vulgaris 'Alba'
Aster (syn. *Symphyotrichum*) 'Little Carlow'

Astrantia 'Claret'
Campanula lactiflora
Campanula lactiflora 'Loddon Anna'
Campanula trachelium 'Alba'
Chaerophyllum hirsutum 'Roseum'
Cimicifuga racemosa 'Atropurpurea'
Clematis 'Alionushka'
Clematis 'Arabella'
Clematis × *bonstedtii* 'Crépuscule'
Clematis flammula 'Sweet Summer Love'
Clematis 'Huldine'
Clematis integrifolia
Clematis 'Margot Koster'
Clematis montana 'Marjorie'
Clematis 'Prince Charles'
Clematis viticella 'Odoriba'
Clematis viticella 'Purpurea Plena Elegans'
Cleome 'Violet Queen'
Cynara cardunculus
Dahlia 'Cornish Ruby'
Dahlia 'Le Baron'
Echinops ritro
Eupatorium purpureum
Euphorbia characias seedlings
Galega × *hartlandii* 'Alba'
Gaura lindheimeri
Geranium sanguineum var. *striatum*
Geranium sylvaticum 'Album'
Geranium sylvaticum 'Mayflower'
Hesperis matronalis

Hydrangea aspera subsp.
  sargentiana
Hydrangea macrophylla
  'White Wave'
Iris 'Cliffs of Dover'
Iris 'Coalignition'
Lunaria annua
Lunaria annua 'Corfu Blue'
Nicotiana mutabilis
  'Marshmallow'
Osteospermum jucundum
  'Langtrees'
Paeonia delavayi × (×
  suffruticosa)
Penstemon 'Countess of
  Dalkeith'
Penstemon digitalis 'Husker
  Red'
Phlox paniculata 'Mount Fuji'
Romneya coulteri
Rosa × *centifolia* 'Fantin Latour'
Rosa 'De Rescht'
Rosa 'Reine des Violettes'
Rosa 'Sheelagh Baird'
Rosa 'Tour de Malakoff'
Salvia 'Amistad'
Salvia 'Magenta Dream'
Salvia × *sylvestris* 'May Night'
Salvia 'Nachvtlinder'
Salvia 'Caradonna'
Salvia 'Peter Vidgeon'
Salvia pratensis 'Indigo'
Sedum (syn. *Hylotelephium*)
  'Matrona'
Stachys byzantina 'Big Ears'
Thalictrum aquilegiifolium
Thalictrum 'Black Stockings'
Thalictrum delavayi
Thalictrum rochebruneanum
Tulipa 'Curly Sue'
Tulipa 'Negrita'
Verbena 'Homestead Purple'

HOLLY HEDGE BORDER

Aconitum carmichaelii
  'Spätlese'
Agapanthus campanulatus
Agapanthus 'Navy Blue'
Agastache foeniculum
Agastache 'Blue Fortune'
Allium cristophii
Alstroemeria (red)
Anemone × *hybrida* 'Honorine
  Jobert'
Anemone × *hybrida* 'Whirlwind'
Aquilegia (pale pink hybrid
  seedling)
Aquilegia clematiflora 'Alba'
Aquilegia vulgaris (pale blue)
Aster × *frikartii* 'Mönch'
Aster (syn. *Symphyotrichum*)
  'Little Carlow'
Aster (syn. *Symphyotrichum*)
  novae-angliae 'Autumn Snow'
Baptisia australis
Campanula lactiflora
Ceanothus × *delileanus*
  'Gloire de Versailles'
Ceanothus × *delileanus*
  'Henri Desfosse'
Cimicifuga racemosa
Clematis × *durandii*
Clematis integrifolia
Clematis 'Marmori'
Dahlia 'Allan Sparkes'
Dahlia 'Karma Serena'
Dahlia merckii
Delphinium 'Blue Jay'
Delphinium 'Faust'
Delphinium 'Finsteraarhorn'
Delphinium 'Summer Skies'
Fuchsia magellanica
  'Mrs Popple'
Galtonia candicans
Hesperantha major

Hesperis matronalis
Hibiscus trionum
Lilium pardalinum
Lobelia tupa
Lythrum salicaria 'Blush'
Narcissus 'Jenny'
Nepeta grandiflora 'Bramdean'
Nicotiana langsdorffii
Nicotiana sylvestris
Nigella damascena
Penstemon 'King George'
Penstemon 'Windsor Red'
Persicaria amplexicaulis 'Alba'
Polemonium caeruleum
  'Album'
Polemonium 'Sonia's Bluebell'
Rosa 'Fred Loads'
Rosa 'Iceberg'
Rosa 'Ispahan'
Rosa 'Jacqueline du Pré'
Rosa 'Scarlet Queen Elizabeth'
Salvia 'Peter Vidgeon'
Salvia 'Silke's Red'
Salvia verticillata 'Purple Rain'
Sedum (syn. *Hylotelephium*)
  spectabile
Sempervivum tectorum
Stachys macrantha
Tulipa 'Finola'
Verbascum chaixii 'Album'
Veronica gentianoides
Veronicastrum virginicum
  'Album'

ROSE GARDEN
Grey bed
Acidanthera bicolor
Agapanthus 'Blue Moon'
Allium 'Purple Sensation'
Campanula lactiflora
Convolvulus cneorum
Diascia fetcaniensis

Fritillaria persica
Heuchera 'Obsidian'
Lavandula 'Munstead'
Orlaya grandiflora
Rosa 'Alfred de Dalmas'
Rosa 'Deep Secret'
Salvia greggii 'Stormy Pink'
Sedum (syn. *Hylotelephium*)
'Bertram Anderson'
Sedum (syn. *Hylotelephium*)
'Matrona'
Stachys byzantina 'Big Ears'
Tulipa 'Exotic Emperor'
Tulipa 'Havran'

Raised bed
Artemisia nutans
Clematis 'Jackmanii Superba'
Clematis 'Perle d'Azur'
Clematis texensis 'Princess
Diana'
Clematis viticella 'Venosa
Violacea'
Convolvulus sabatius
Dianthus 'Coconut Sundae'
Diascia integerrima
Diascia vigilis
Heuchera 'Obsidian'
Heuchera 'Palace Purple'
Iris stylosa
Lilium regale
Nepeta racemosa
Nerine bowdenii
Omphalodes linifolia
Penstemon 'Apple Blossom'
Penstemon 'Hidcote Pink'
Rosa 'Apple Blossom'
Rosa 'Cornelia'
Rosa 'Goldfinch'
Rosa 'Little White Pet'
Rosa 'Macmillan Nurse'
Salvia 'Penny's Smile'

Sarcococca humilis
Sedum (syn. *Hylotelephium*)
'Coca Cola'
Sedum (syn. *Hylotelephium*)
'Ruby Glow'
Senecio viravira
Tulipa 'Elegant Lady'
Tulipa 'Havran'
Verbascum chaixii 'Album'

Former rose beds
Acidanthera bicolor
Agapanthus africanus 'Alba'
Agapanthus 'Blue Moon'
Antirrhinum 'Black Prince'
Campanula lactiflora
Caryopteris × *clandonensis*
'Heavenly Blue'
Cleome 'Cherry Queen'
Eryngium bourgatii
Eryngium bourgatii 'Picos
Blue'
Erysimum 'Constant Cheer'
Geranium renardii
Heuchera 'Chocolate Ruffles'
Iris pallida 'Argentea
Variegata'
Lavandula 'Silver Sands'
Libertia grandiflora (syn. *L.
chilensis*)
Lilium regale
Orlaya grandiflora
Paeonia 'Duchesse de
Nemours'
Paeonia 'Sarah Bernhardt'
Phillyrea angustifolia
Rosa 'Deep Secret'
Rosa 'The Fairy'
Rosa 'Little White Pet'
Salvia 'African Skies'
Salvia 'Penny's Smile'
Salvia verticillata 'Purple Rain'

Sedum (syn. *Hylotelephium*)
'Bertram Anderson'
Sedum (syn. *Hylotelephium*)
'Matrona'
Tulipa 'Black Hero'
Tulipa 'Elegant Lady'

Rose Garden general
Alstroemeria 'Princess
Frederika'
Anisodontea 'El Rayo'
Cardamine waldsteinii
Carpenteria californica
Clematis 'Huldine'
Clematis texensis 'Princess
Diana'
Dahlia 'Gerri Hoek'
Dahlia 'Labyrinth'
Diascia fetcaniensis
Eryngium × *oliverianum*
Euphorbia myrsinites
Galanthus 'Jacquenetta'
Galanthus plicatus ex Coton
Manor
Geranium endressii 'Wargrave
Pink'
Geranium renardii 'Phillip
Vapelle'
Heuchera 'Berry Smoothie'
Hydrangea arborescens
'Annabelle'
Lavandula 'Munstead'
Meconopsis (unnamed)
Narcissus cyclamineus 'Jenny'
Orlaya grandiflora
Paeonia delavayi ×
(× *suffruticosa*)
Paeonia emodi
Paeonia mlokosewitschii
Penstemon 'Apple Blossom'
Penstemon 'Hidcote Pink'
Rosa 'Cornelia'

Rosa 'The Fairy'
Rosa 'Ghislaine de Féligonde'
Rosa 'Glyndebourne'
Rosa 'Gruss an Aachen'
Rosa 'Mrs Oakley Fisher'
Rosa 'Phyllis Bide'
Salvia 'Amistad'
Salvia 'Javier'
Tulipa 'Elegant Lady'
Tulipa 'Exotic Emperor'
Tulipa 'Havran'

MEDITERRANEAN BANK
Achillea 'Salmon Beauty'
Agapanthus 'Dr Brouwer'
Agapanthus Headbourne
   hybrids
Agapanthus 'Sandringham'
Allium cristophii
Anthericum liliago
Asphodelus albus
Buddleja colvilei
Buddleja salviifolia
Cerinthe major 'Purpurascens'
Cistus 'Grayswood Pink'
Cistus (unnamed)
Clematis heracleifolia
   'Cassandra'
Clematis × jouiniana
Diascia integerrima
Diascia vigilis
Eryngium agavifolium
Eryngium bourgatii
Erysimum 'Constant Cheer'
Euphorbia characias hybrid
Euphorbia dulcis 'Chamaeleon'
Euphorbia myrsinites
Euphorbia stygiana
Galanthus nivalis
Geranium 'Orion'
Geranium 'Rozanne'
Geum 'Coral Supreme'

Geum 'Totally Tangerine'
Hebe salicifolia 'Spender's
   Seedling'
Heuchera 'Amethyst'
Heuchera 'Palace Purple'
Heuchera 'Plum Pudding'
Iris 'Broadleigh Rose'
Iris 'Deep Black'
Iris 'Langport Wren'
Iris (mauve)
Lavandula 'Hidcote'
Lavandula 'Munstead'
Libertia grandiflora
   (syn. L. chilensis)
Nepeta 'Six Hills Giant'
Olea europaea
Paeonia 'Copper Kettle'
   (Itoh hybrid)
Paeonia 'Duchesse de
   Nemours'
Paradisea lusitanica
Parahebe perfoliata
Phlomis italica
Potentilla × hopwoodiana
Rosa glauca
Rosa 'Lady Emma Hamilton'
Rosa 'Lady of Shalott'
Rosa 'The Lark Ascending'
Rosa 'Louise Clements'
Rosa 'Meg'
Rosa 'Mrs Oakley Fisher'
Rosa 'Sally Holmes'
Rosmarinus officinalis 'Miss
   Jessopp's Upright'
Salvia 'Javier'
Salvia 'Purple Queen'
Salvia 'Rimambelle'
Salvia 'Salmon'
Salvia 'Señorita Leah'
Salvia 'Trelawny Rose Pink'
Sedum (syn. Hylotelephium)
   'Bertram Anderson'

Sedum (syn. Hylotelephium)
   'Hab Grey'
Sedum (syn. Hylotelephium)
   'Purple Emperor'
Sedum (syn. Hylotelephium)
   'Red Cauli'
Sedum (syn. Hylotelephium)
   telephium subsp. ruprechtii
Thymus doerfleri
Tulipa bakeri 'Lilac Wonder'
Tulipa 'Jimmy'
Tulipa 'Request'
Tulipa saxatilis

ROSE BANK
Achillea ageratum
   'W. B. Childs'
Achillea millefolium 'Cassis'
Achillea millefolium 'Cerise
   Queen'
Achillea millefolium 'Cherry
   King'
Allium nigrum
Allium sphaerocephalon
Anaphalis triplinervis
   'Summer Snow'
Anemone × hybrida 'Honorine
   Jobert'
Anemone × hybrida 'Queen
   Charlotte'
Antirrhinum 'Black Prince'
Antirrhinum majus 'Admiral
   White'
Aquilegia vulgaris
Aquilegia vulgaris 'Heidi'
Artemisia alba 'Canescens'
Artemisia nutans
Aster amellus 'King George'
Aster thomsonii 'Nanus'
Ballota pseudodictamnus
Buddleja crispa
Buddleja 'Lochinch'

Campanula lactiflora
Centaurea dealbata
Ceratostigma plumbaginoides
Clematis 'Arabella'
Clematis heracleifolia
  'Cassandra'
Clematis 'Romantika'
Clematis viticella 'Polish Spirit'
Cleome 'White Queen'
Colchicum 'Waterlily'
Commelina coelestis
Crinum × powellii
Dianthus carthusianorum
Dianthus 'Coconut Sundae'
Dianthus 'Laced Monarch'
Drimys aromatica
Echinacea purpurea 'Magnus'
Echinacea purpurea 'Rubinstern'
Eryngium bourgatii
Eryngium giganteum
Eryngium pandanifolium
Euphorbia characias subsp.
  wulfenii hybrids
Francoa ramosa
Gaura lindheimeri
Geranium 'Anne Thomson'
Geranium × cantabrigiense
  'Biokovo'
Geranium clarkei 'Kashmir
  White'
Geranium libani
Geranium × oxonianum
  'Walter's Gift'
Geranium palmatum
Geranium 'Patricia'
Geranium pratense 'Mrs Kendall
  Clark'
Geranium × riversleaianum
  'Mavis Simpson'
Geranium × riversleaianum
  'Russell Prichard'
Gladiolus papilio 'Ruby'

Iris 'Elegans' (our own name
  for an inherited iris)
Iris 'Jane Phillips'
Iris 'Midnight Skies'(our own
  name for an inherited iris)
Iris 'Quechee'
Leucanthemum × superbum
  'Alaska'
Lunaria rediviva
Melianthus major
Nepeta racemosa
Nepeta 'Six Hills Giant'
Paeonia 'Blue Lotus'
Paeonia 'Cora Louise'
Paeonia (deep pink)
Paeonia delavayi ×
  (× suffruticosa)
Paeonia 'Duchesse de Nemours'
Paeonia 'Hillary'
Paeonia rockii hybrid
Paeonia rockii hybrid seedling
Paeonia × suffruticosa
  'Double White'
Paeonia 'Watermelon Wine'
Papaver orientale 'Cedric
  Morris'
Papaver orientale 'Royal
  Wedding'
Penstemon 'Abbotsmerry'
Penstemon 'Apple Blossom'
Penstemon 'Garnet'
Perovskia atriplicifolia
  'Blue Spire'
Rosa 'Alan Titchmarsh'
Rosa 'Bonica'
Rosa 'Charles de Mills'
Rosa 'De Rescht'
Rosa 'Ellen Willmott'
Rosa 'Empress Josephine'
Rosa 'Fantin-Latour'
Rosa 'Felicia'
Rosa 'Ferdinand Pichard'

Rosa gallica 'Versicolor'
Rosa 'Gertrude Jekyll'
Rosa 'Hermosa'
Rosa 'Kazanlik'
Rosa 'Königin von Dänemark'
Rosa 'Little White Pet'
Rosa 'Louise Odier'
Rosa 'Madame Isaac Péreire'
Rosa 'Madame Pierre Oger'
Rosa 'Olivia Rose Austin'
Rosa 'Pearl Drift'
Rosa 'Penelope'
Rosa pimpinellifolia
Rosa 'Prosperity'
Rosa 'Quatre Saisons'
Rosa 'Redouté'
Rosa rugosa 'Blanc Double de
  Coubert'
Rosa rugosa 'Belle Poitevine'
Rosa rugosa 'Fimbriata'
Rosa rugosa 'Fru Dagmar
  Hastrup'
Rosa rugosa 'Hansa'
Rosa 'Scepter'd Isle'
Rosa 'Sheelagh Baird'
Rosa 'Souvenir de la Malmaison'
Rosa 'Souvenir de Malmédy'
Rosa 'St Ethelburga'
Salvia 'Caradonna'
Salvia interrupta
Salvia involucrata
Salvia microphylla 'Pink Blush'
Salvia microphylla 'Cerro Potosi'
Salvia patens
Salvia 'Peter Vidgeon'
Salvia 'Purple Queen'
Salvia 'Stormy Pink'
Salvia × sylvestris 'Blauhügel'
Salvia × sylvestris 'May Night'
Saponaria × lempergii 'Max Frei'
Sedum (syn. Hylotelephium)
  'Carl'

Sedum (syn. *Hylotelephium*)
   'Frosty Morn'
Sedum (syn. *Hylotelephium*)
   'Joyce Henderson'
Sedum (syn. *Hylotelephium*)
   'Purple Emperor'
Sesseli libanotis
Syringa meyeri 'Palibin'
Valeriana phu 'Aurea'
Verbascum chaixii 'Album'
Verbascum 'Pink Domino'

MIDSUMMER BORDER
Upper side
Althaea armeniaca
Amsonia tabernaemontana
Anaphalis triplinervis
Anemone × hybrida 'Queen
   Charlotte'
Aster (syn. *Symphyotrichum*)
   ericoides
Aster × frikartii 'Mönch'
Aster (syn. *Symphyotrichum*)
   laeve 'Calliope'
Aster (syn. *Symphyiotrichum*)
   laterifolius var. *horizontalis*
Aster (syn. *Symphyotrichum*)
   'Little Carlow'
Astrantia major 'Margery Fish'
Campanula glomerata
   'Superba'
Campanula lactiflora
Campanula lactiflora 'Loddon
   Anna'
Campanula trachelium
   'Bernice'
Chelone obliqua
Cimicifuga racemosa
Cimicifuga simplex var.
   simplex 'Brunette'
Clematis 'Black Prince'
Clematis × durandii

Clematis heracleifolia
   'Cassandra'
Clematis viticella 'Madame
   Julia Correvon'
Clematis 'Petit Faucon'
Clematis 'Vyvyan Pennell'
Cleome 'Violet Queen'
Dahlia 'Allan Sparkes'
Dahlia 'Shaggy Pink'
Dahlia sherffii
Delphinium 'Black Knight'
Delphinium 'Finsteraarhorn'
Echinacea purpurea
Echinacea purpurea
   'White Swan'
Eupatorium purpureum
Francoa racemosa
Geranium 'Mrs Kendall Clark'
Geranium 'Patricia'
Geranium psilostemon
Geranium sanguineum 'Elke'
Geranium sylvaticum
   'Mayflower'
Iris (pink)
Iris (plum)
Iris sibirica 'Pearl Queen'
Lathyrus latifolius 'Albus'
Lythrum salicaria
Lythrum salicaria 'Blush'
Monarda 'Deep Pink'
Monarda 'Prairie Night'
Monarda 'Violet Queen'
Nicotiana mutabilis
   'Marshmallow'
Penstemon 'Countess of
   Dalkeith'
Phlox 'Luc's Lilac'
Phlox paniculata 'Mount Fuji'
Phlox 'Utopia'
Rosa 'Cardinal de Richelieu'
Rosa 'Climbing Iceberg'
Rosa 'Comte de Chambord'

Rosa 'De Rescht'
Rosa 'Pearl Drift'
Rosa 'Rosy Cushion'
Rosa 'Tess of the d'Urbervilles'
Rosa 'Tuscany Superb'
Rosa 'William Lobb'
Salvia involucrata
Thalictrum 'Thundercloud'
Verbascum chaixii 'Album'
Veronica longifolia
Veronica spicata 'Pink Damask'
Veronicastrum virginicum
   'Album'
Veronicastrum virginicum
   'Fascination'
Veronicastrum virginicum
   'Lavendelturm'

Lower side
Acer griseum
Achillea 'Cerise Queen'
Aconitum carmichaelii
   'Kelmscott'
Aconitum napellus
Althaea armeniaca
Amsonia (syn. *Rhazya*)
   orientalis
Anaphalis 'Summer Snow'
Aster × frikartii 'Mönch'
Anemone × hybrida
   'Queen Charlotte'
Bidens heterophylla
Campanula lactiflora
Centaurea montana 'Alba'
Chelone obliqua
Chrysanthemum uliginosum
Clematis × durandii
Clematis heracleifolia
   'Cassandra'
Clematis 'Minuet'
Clematis 'Semu'
Cleome 'Violet Queen'

Dahlia 'Allan Sparkes'
Dahlia 'Shaggy Pink'
Dahlia sherffii
Delphinium 'Black Knight'
Delphinium elatum
   'Finsteraarhorn'
Echinacea purpurea
Echinacea purpurea 'Magnus'
Eupatorium purpureum
   'Atropurpureum'
Francoa racemosa
Geranium × magnificum
Geranium 'Nimbus'
Geranium 'Patricia'
Geranium pratense 'Plenum
   Violaceum'
Geranium 'Sirak'
Helleborus 'Magic Leaves'
Iris (mauve)
Iris (pale mauve)
Iris (plum)
Iris sibirica 'Silver Edge'
Knautia macedonica
Liquidambar styraciflua
Lobelia 'Hadspen Purple'
Lupinus 'The Governor'
Lythrum salicaria 'Blush'
Lythrum salicaria 'Dropmore
   Purple'
Monarda 'Violet Queen'
Nepeta 'Bramdean'
Penstemon 'Apple Blossom'
Persicaria bistorta 'Superba'
Phlox paniculata 'Blue
   Paradise'
Phlox paniculata 'Hesperis'
Phlox paniculata 'Luc's Lilac'
Phlox paniculata 'Mount Fuji'
Rosa 'Blush Noisette'
Rosa 'Louise Odier'
Rosa 'Munstead Wood'
Rosa 'Our Beth'

Rosa 'Prince Charles'
Rosa 'William Lobb'
Rosa 'William Shakespeare'
Rosa 'Zigeunerknabe'
Salvia 'Blush Pink'
Salvia involucrata
Sedum (syn. Hylotelephium)
   'Frosty Morn'
Sedum (syn. Hylotelephium)
   'Matrona'
Sedum (syn. Hylotelephium)
   spectabile
Sidalcea 'Elsie Heugh'
Thalictrum rochebruneanum
Thalictrum 'Splendide White'
Vernonia crinita
Veronicastrum virginicum
   'Fascination'
Veronicastrum virginicum
   'Lavendelturm'
Veronicastrum virginicum
   'Pink Glow'

RED BORDER
Achillea 'Cloth of Gold'
Achillea 'Paprika'
Achillea 'Red Velvet'
Alstroemeria psittacina
Bidens heterophylla
Crocosmia 'Lucifer'
Dahlia 'Bishop of Auckland'
Dahlia 'Bishop of Llandaff'
Dahlia 'Bishop's Stepdaughter'
Dahlia 'Ragged Robin'
Dahlia 'Rip City'
Dahlia 'Shooting Star'
Dahlia 'Witteman's Best'
Echinacea 'Green Jewel'
Echinacea 'Jade'
Echinacea 'White Swan'
Euphorbia ceratocarpa
Euphorbia schillingii

Euphorbia wallichii
Fuchsia magellanica 'Aurea'
Geum 'Mrs Bradshaw'
Iris 'Elegans' (our own name
   for an inherited iris)
Iris sibirica 'White Swirl'
Kniphofia 'Bees' Lemon'
Kniphofia 'Jade'
Kniphofia 'Percy's Pride'
Lupinus 'Chandelier'
Monarda 'Gardenview Scarlet'
Nepeta govaniana
Nicotiana 'Lime Green'
Papaver 'Beauty of Livermore'
Penstemon 'King George'
Persicaria amplexicaulis
   'Fat Domino'
Potentilla 'Gibson's Scarlet'
Potentilla 'Monsieur Rouillard'
Rosa 'Albéric Barbier'
Rosa 'Buff Beauty'
Rosa 'Dublin Bay'
Rosa 'Imogen'
Salvia microphylla var.
   neurepia
Salvia 'Royal Bumble'
Salvia 'Sungold'
Scabiosa columbaria subsp.
   ochroleleuca
Selinum wallichianum
Tulipa 'Maja'

BLUE AND YELLOW
BORDER
Upper side
Achillea filipendula 'Cloth of
   Gold'
Achillea 'Inca Gold'
Aconitum × arendsii
Aconitum carmichaelii
   'Spätlese'
Agastache 'Blue Fortune

Alstroemeria 'Yellow
  Friendship'
Amsonia (syn. *Rhazya*)
  orientalis
Aster (syn. *Symphyotrichum*)
  'Little Carlow'
Bidens heterophylla
Caltha palustris var. 'Alba'
Clematis 'Black Prince'
Clematis heracleifolia
  'Cassandra'
Dahlia 'Bishop of Coton'
  (our own name)
Dahlia 'Café au Lait'
Delphinium 'Black Knight'
Delphinium 'Faust'
Digitalis lutea
Geranium pratense 'Mrs
  Kendall Clark'
Hemerocallis fulva 'Flore
  Pleno'
Hosta fortunei
Iris ensata
Iris 'Gerald Darby'
Iris 'Paul's Purple'
Iris sibirica 'Ruffled Velvet'
Ligularia dentata 'Desdemona'
Osmunda regalis
Paeonia lutea var. *ludlowii*
Phlomis russeliana
Primula florindae
Rosa 'Buff Beauty'
Rosa 'Maigold'
Rosa 'Sweet Juliet'
Rudbeckia fulgida var. *deamii*
Rudbeckia 'Green Wizard'
Salvia 'Amistad'
Salvia 'Sungold'
Tulipa 'Maja'
Verbena bonariensis
Zantedeschia 'Green Goddess'

Lower side
Achillea 'Inca Gold'
Achillea 'Moonshine'
Aconitum × arendsii
Aconitum carmichaelii
  'Kelmscott'
Aconitum carmichaelii
  'Spätlese'
Alcea rugosa
Alstroemeria 'Yellow
  Friendship'
Amsonia (syn. *Rhazya*)
  orientalis
Aster × frikartii 'Wunder von
  Stafa'
Baptisia australis
Campanula lactiflora
  'Prichard's Variety'
Campanula 'Sarastro'
Clematis 'Black Prince'
Clematis heracleifolia
  'Cassandra'
Dahlia 'Banana Cabana'
Dahlia 'Glorie van Noordwijk'
Dahlia 'Shooting Star'
Delphinium 'Black Knight'
Delphinium 'Faust'
Digitalis ferruginea
Euphorbia wallichii
Geranium × magnificum
Geranium 'Nimbus'
Geranium pratense 'Mrs
  Kendall Clark'
Helenium 'Sahin's Early
  Flowerer'
Helianthus 'Lemon Queen'
Hemerocallis 'Cream Drop'
Hemerocallis dumorteri
Hypericum × inodorum
  'Elstead'
Iris 'Dusky Skies' (our own
  name for an inherited iris)

Iris 'Rajah'
Kniphofia 'Green Jade'
Kniphofia 'Percy's Pride'
Kniphofia 'Wrexham Buttercup'
Lupinus 'Chandelier'
Lupinus 'The Governor'
Lysimachia ciliata 'Firecracker'
Nepeta subsessilis
Potentilla fruticosa
  'Vilmoriniana'
Rosa 'Autumn Sunset'
Rosa 'Golden Wings'
Rosa 'Imogen'
Rosa 'Maigold'
Rudbeckia 'Goldsturm'
Salvia 'Caradonna'
Salvia × sylvestris 'May Night'
Salvia × sylvestris 'Viola Klose'
Selinum wallichianum
Thalictrum flavum subsp.
  glaucum
Tulipa 'Maja'
Thermopsis lanceolata
Verbena bonariensis

MEADOW BORDER
Achillea 'Inca Gold'
Achillea 'Terracotta'
Aconitum carmichaelii
  'Kelmscott'
Aconitum carmichaelii
  'Spätlese'
Agastache 'Blue Fortune'
Agastache foeniculum
Amsonia 'Ernst Pagels'
Amsonia hubrichtii
Aster amellus 'King George'
Aster × frikartii 'Jungfrau'
Aster × frikartii 'Wunder von
  Stafe'
Aster (syn. *Symphyotrichum*)
  laeve 'Calliope'

Aster (syn. *Symphyotrichum*)
'Little Carlow'
Buddleja lindleyana
Campanula lactiflora
Centaurea montana
Crocosmia 'Zambesi'
Dahlia 'Glorie van Noordwijk'
Digitalis parviflora
Digitalis parviflora 'Milk
Chocolate'
Echinacea purpurea 'Magnus'
Echinops bannaticus 'Taplow
Blue'
Eupatorium rugosum
'Chocolate'
Geranium × magnificum
Geranium 'Rozanne'
Geum 'Prinses Juliana'
Geum 'Totally Tangerine'
Helenium 'Sahin's Early
Flowerer'
Helenium 'Septemberfuchs'
Helenium 'Zimbelstern'
Kniphofia 'Brimstone'
Kniphofia caulescens
Kniphofia 'Green Jade'
Kniphofia rooperi
Kniphofia 'Tawny King'
Kniphofia 'Tetbury Torch'
Ligularia dentata 'Desdemona'
Lythrum salicaria
Nepeta 'Six Hills Giant'
Papaver orientale
Perovskia atriplicifolia
'Blue Spire'
Potentilla russelliana 'William
Rollison'
Tagetes 'Cinnabar'
Tulipa 'Ballerina'
Verbena bonariensis

HERB GARDEN
Key:
C = Culinary use
D = Dyeing use
M = Medicinal use
Achillea ageratifolia (Balkan
yarrow) M
Achillea decolorans (English
mace) C
Aconitum lycoctonum subsp.
vulparia (wolf's bane) M
Aconitum napellus (monk's
hood) M
Agrimonia eupatoria (agrimony)
M
Ajuga reptans 'Atropurpurea'
(bugle) M
Angelica archangelica (garden
angelica) CM
Aquilegia vulgaris (common
columbine) M
Artemisia abrotanum
(southernwood) M
Aremisia absinthium 'Lambrook
Silver' (wormwood) M
Artemisia vulgaris (mugwort) M
Borago officinalis (borage) C
Buxus sempervirens 'Suffruticosa'
(boxwood) M
Calendula officinalis (pot
marigold) M
Cedronella canariensis (balm of
Gilead) M
Centaurea cyanus (cornflower) M
Chamomile 'Treneague' (lawn
chamomile) M
Chenopodium bonus-henricus
(good King Henry) C
Chenopodium rubrum (red
goosefoot) C
Cynoglossum officinale (hound's
tongue) M

Digitalis grandiflora (large
yellow foxglove) M
Digitalis lutea (straw foxglove)
M
Digitalis purpurea (common
foxglove) M
Echinacea purpurea (purple
coneflower) M
Echium vulgare (viper's bugloss)
M
Eryngium giganteum (Miss
Willmott's ghost) M
Foeniculum vulgare (common
fennel) C
Fumaria officinalis (common
fumitory) M
Genista tinctoria (dyer's
greenweed) D
Hyoscyamus niger (black
henbane) M
Hypericum perforatum (St John's
wort) M
Hyssopus officinalis (hyssop)
CM
Hyssopus offinalis 'Roseus' (pink
hyssop) CM
Inula helenium (elecampane) M
Iris 'Elegans' (our own name for
an inherited iris) M
Isatis tinctoria (woad) D
Lavandula dentata (French
lavender) M
Lavandula 'Munstead' (English
lavender) M
Levisticum officinale (lovage) C
Lippia citriodora (syn. *Aloysia
triphylla*) (lemon verbena) C
Lithospermum officinale
(common gromwell) M
Lonicera periclymenum
'Graham Thomas'
(honeysuckle) M

Lycopus europaeus (gypsywort) M

Mandragora officinarum (common mandrake) M

Melilotus officinalis (sweet clover) M

Melissa officinalis 'Aurea' (golden lemon balm) CM

Mentha × *gentilis* 'Variegata' (variegated ginger mint) CM

Mentha × *gracilis* (ginger mint) CM

Mentha longifolia (horse mint) CM

Mentha × *piperita* (peppermint) CM

Mentha spicata (common mint) CM

Mentha suaveolens 'Variegata' (variegated apple mint) CM

Meum athamanticum (bald money) M

Monarda citriodora (bergamot) CM

Myrrhis odorata (sweet cicely) C

Nepeta × *faassenii* (catmint) M

Nigella damascena (love-in-a-mist) M

Onopordum acanthium (Scottish thistle) M

Origanum 'Hopley's Purple' (ornamental marjoram) CM

Origanum vulgare (English marjoram) CM

Origanum vulgare 'Aureum' (golden marjoram) CM

Papaver somniferum (opium poppy) M

Phytolacca americana (American pokeweed) M

Rosa rugosa 'Alba' (white Japanese rose) M

Rosmarinus officinalis 'Miss Jessopp's Upright' (rosemary) C

Rubia tinctorum (madder) D

Rumex acetosa (common sorrel) C

Ruta graveolens 'Jackman's Blue' (rue) M

Salvia elegans (pineapple sage) C

Salvia lavandulifolia (lavender-leaved sage) CM

Salvia officinalis (common sage) CM

Salvia officinalis 'Purpurascens' (purple sage) CM

Salvia sclarea var. *turkestanica* (clary sage) M

Satureja montana (winter savory) C

Scutellaria lateriflora (skullcap) M

Smyrnium perfoliatum (perfoliate alexanders) C

Stachys officinalis (betony) M

Symphytum grandiflorum 'Goldsmith' (comfrey) M

Tanacetum balsamita (alecost) CM

Tanacetum parthenium (feverfew) M

Teucrium chamaedrys (germander) M

Thymus citriodorus (lemon thyme) C

Thymus 'Doone Valley' (garden thyme) C

Thymus serpyllum (creeping thyme) C

Thymus serpyllum 'Goldstream' (creeping thyme) C

Thymus vulgaris 'Silver Posie' (silver thyme) C

Verbena officinalis (vervain) M

Vitex agnus-castus (chaste tree)

Index

Lycopus europaeus (gypsywort)
M

Mandragora officinarum
(common mandrake) M

Melilotus officinalis (sweet
clover) M

Melissa officinalis 'Aurea'
(golden lemon balm) CM

Mentha × gentilis 'Variegata'
(variegated ginger mint) CM

Mentha × gracilis (ginger mint)
CM

Mentha longifolia (horse mint)
CM

Mentha × piperita (peppermint)
CM

Mentha spicata (common mint)
CM

Mentha suaveolens 'Variegata'
(variegated apple mint) CM

Meum athamanticum (bald
money) M

Monarda citriodora (bergamot)
CM

Myrrhis odorata (sweet cicely) C

Nepeta × faassenii (catmint) M

Nigella damascena (love-in-a-
mist) M

Onopordum acanthium
(Scottish thistle) M

Origanum 'Hopley's Purple'
(ornamental marjoram) CM

Origanum vulgare (English
marjoram) CM

Origanum vulgare 'Aureum'
(golden marjoram) CM

Papaver somniferum (opium
poppy) M

Phytolacca americana
(American pokeweed) M

Rosa rugosa 'Alba' (white
Japanese rose) M

Rosmarinus officinalis
'Miss Jessopp's Upright'
(rosemary) C

Rubia tinctorum (madder) D

Rumex acetosa (common
sorrel) C

Ruta graveolens 'Jackman's
Blue' (rue) M

Salvia elegans (pineapple sage)
C

Salvia lavandulifolia (lavender-
leaved sage) CM

Salvia officinalis (common
sage) CM

Salvia officinalis
'Purpurascens' (purple sage)
CM

Salvia sclarea var. *turkestanica*
(clary sage) M

Satureja montana (winter
savory) C

Scutellaria lateriflora (skullcap)
M

Smyrnium perfoliatum
(perfoliate alexanders) C

Stachys officinalis (betony) M

Symphytum grandiflorum
'Goldsmith' (comfrey) M

Tanacetum balsamita (alecost)
CM

Tanacetum parthenium
(feverfew) M

Teucrium chamaedrys
(germander) M

Thymus citriodorus (lemon
thyme) C

Thymus 'Doone Valley' (garden
thyme) C

Thymus serpyllum (creeping
thyme) C

Thymus serpyllum 'Goldstream'
(creeping thyme) C

Thymus vulgaris 'Silver Posie'
(silver thyme) C

Verbena officinalis (vervain) M

Vitex agnus-castus (chaste
tree)

Index

Note: Page numbers in *italics* refer to images. Only major plant types have been included here. Plant genera/species are listed on pages 228–237.

Acknowledgements

AUTHOR'S ACKNOWLEDGEMENTS

I would like to thank both Andrew Lawson and Griselda Kerr for introducing me to Pimpernel Press. I am eternally grateful to Pimpernel's Publisher, Jo Christian, and Managing Director, Gail Lynch, for generously agreeing to publish my book. And my gratitude extends to Nancy Marten for her skill and patience in editing the text and to Anne Wilson for her marvellous design work in bringing the book to fruition. I must also thank Nicola Stocken, Michael Simon, Tom Malone and Thyago de Souza for allowing their beautiful photographs to be used to illustrate the book. I am also deeply grateful to Andrew Lawson for his generous Foreword, which captures the essence of the book.

I would never have been able to carry out the work in a garden this size without the help of some very key people, one or two of whom are mentioned in the book. Richard Green, our Head Gardener, has worked at Coton since 1979 and has proved the most loyal, creative and multi-talented person that any garden owner could wish for. For twenty-three years Michael Simon gardened alongside him and helped with some of the major changes we carried out in the early years of our tenure. The late John Kimball gave us eight invaluable years before retiring in the late 1990s, as did Sue Hill, who worked here for eight years before emigrating to New Zealand. Fortunately for me her place was taken by Sue Mappledorham in 2006 and Sue has remained my invaluable soulmate in the garden when it comes to having a sounding board for ideas. I have also received wonderful gardening help from Catharina Hunter, Teddy Cripps, Katherine Clarke, Liz Reader and Thyago de Souza over the years, not forgetting the excellent team who work in our Potting Shed producing plants for sale in the Nursery and use in the garden. Finally, I would like to thank my husband, Ian, for his encouragement and forbearance in allowing my passion for gardening to occasionally impinge on domestic responsibilities.

PICTURE CREDITS
PHOTOGRAPHS
All photographs by Susie Pasley-Tyler except:
Tom Malone: pages 106, 110–11, 190–91, 211 (bottom right)
Michael Simon: pages 19 (left), 20 (left), 23 (top left, top right), 29 (below right), 31 (right), 33 (above left), 34, 35 (above and below), 77 (bottom right), 79 (top), 103 (bottom left), 109 (centre), 121 (top right), 126–7, 131 (top right), 132, 133, 139, 142–3, 146, 161 (top right), 165, 179 (left), 187, 194–5, 198 (right), 199 (right), 205 (top left and centre left)
Thyago de Souza: page 33 (bottom)
Nicola Stocken: title page, pages 22, 25 (bottom right), 28, 29 (bottom left), 30 (top right and bottom right), 31 (left), 38–9, 44–5, 56–7, 67, 69 (bottom), 72, 77 (top left), 81 (top left, bottom right, bottom left), 156 (bottom left), 207 (top right and bottom left)
ILLUSTRATIONS
By kind permission of Andrew Lawson: page 18
Chris Prout: page 8
Jane Simon: pages 14–15